PENCIL POWER

Illustrators can have a rather solitary existence. Tucked away in their studios they while away the hours doodling, waiting for that phone to ring...

...And when it does ring it's the usual crisis. Like Clark Kent, they spring into action – with no time to lose as someone's job is on the line.

Images **27** gathers together some of the most dazzling assignments completed during the year.

They may be solitary but those guys on the end of the phone are special people.

Images 27 published by
The Association of Illustrators
81 Leonard Street London EC2A 4QS
T +44 (0) 20 7613 4328
E info@a-o-illustrators.demon.co.uk
W www.theAOI.com

Book designed by Atelier Works

Production in Hong Kong by
Hong Kong Graphics and Printing Ltd
T (852) 2976 0289
F (852) 2976 0292

Acknowledgements
We are grateful for the support of the many organisations
and individuals who contribute to the Images exhibition
and annual:

Our dedicated team of judges for applying their expertise
to the difficult task of selecting this year's work

The Mall Galleries for hosting the Images 27 Exhibition

Pentagram Design Ltd for their kind support of Images 27
through The Pentagram Award

Rachel Goslin for the use of her illustrations with the
annual and on the Call for Entries form

Finers Stephens Innocent for their legal advice

Nicole Peli for the production of Images 27

Ian Chilvers and Joe Luffman at Atelier Works for their design

All our dedicated casual staff and volunteers for their
invaluable assistance with the competition and exhibition

The Association of Illustrators
AOI Volunteer Council of Management: Francis Blake,
Michael Bramman, Joanne Davies, Leo Duff, Adam Graff,
Willi Gray, Rod Hunt, Alison Lang

Advisors: Stuart Briers, Edward Eaves, Ruth Gladwin,
Robert Lands, James Marsh, Beth Pountney, Simon Stern,
Fig Taylor

Exhibitions and Events: Harriet Booth (to Feb 03)
T +44 (0) 20 7739 8901

Project Co-ordinator: Rochelle Symons (from Feb 03)
T +44 (0) 20 7739 8901

Membership and Publications: Anna Steinberg,
Matt Johnson & Derek Brazell
T +44 (0) 20 7613 4328

Accounts: Paul Hobgen, Ventura BHP
T +44 (0)1622 844 417

contents

about the **AOI**

The AOI was established in 1973 to advance and protect illustrator's rights and encourage professional standards. The AOI is a non-profit making trade association dedicated to its members' professional interests and the promotion of illustration.

Members consist primarily of freelance illustrators as well as agents, clients, students and lecturers. The AOI is run by an administrative staff responsible to a volunteer Council of Management.

Campaigning

As the only body to represent illustrators and campaign for their rights in the UK, the AOI has successfully increased the standing of illustration as a profession and improved the commercial and ethical conditions of employment for illustrators. The AOI is a member of the Creators Rights Alliance (CRA), and the British Copyright Council (BCC). It helped to establish the secondary rights arm of the Designers and Artists Copyright Society, (DACS), the UK visual arts collecting society.

Responsible for establishing the right of illustrators to retain ownership of their artwork the AOI aims to expose and resist rights abuses and exploitative practices within the industry whenever they occur. On behalf of its members, and with their continued support, the AOI can attempt things that would be difficult or impossible individually. As part of the CRA, for example, the AOI is able to lobby parliament for changes in UK law, aligning it more closely with those of our European neighbours, widely seen as more creator friendly. We are also commissioning further research into the extent of creators rights abuses, with a view to challenging the DCMS, and examining the shortcomings of the new communications bill from a creator's perspective.

Information and support services

Portfolio advice

Members are entitled to a free annual consultation with the AOI's portfolio consultant. Objective advice is given on portfolio presentation and content, suitable illustration markets and agents.

Journal

The AOI Journal is distributed bi-monthly to members, keeping them informed about exhibitions, competitions, campaigns and activities in the profession. Also available to non-members on subscription.

Hotline advice

Members have access to a special Hotline number if they need advice about pricing commissions, copyright and ethics problems.

Publications

The AOI publishes Rights: The Illustrator's Guide to Professional Practice, a comprehensive guide to the law for illustrators. It provides detailed advice on how

to protect against exploitative practices and contains a model contract for illustrators to use. We also produce Survive: The Illustrator's Guide to a Professional Career which is a comprehensive practical guide to beginning and continuing a career as a professional illustrator. Survive includes information about marketing, ethics, agents and a guide to fees. These publications are available to members at reduced rates.

Client directories

The AOI currently has three illustration client directories. The Editorial Directory has details of over 120 contacts in the newspaper and magazine industries. The Publishing Directory is a comprehensive list of over 170 important contacts in book publishing. The Advertising Directory has details of over 150 contacts from the world of advertising.

Business advice

Members are entitled to a free consultation with the AOI Chartered Accountant, who can advise on accounting, National Insurance, tax, VAT and book-keeping.

Regional groups

The contact details of regional representatives, who organise social activities for regional members and provide an important support network, are listed in the Journal.

Discounts

Members receive discounts on AOI events, publications and a number of art material suppliers nationwide.

Legal advice

Full and Associate members receive advice on ethics and contractual problems, copyright and moral right disputes.

Return of artwork stickers

Available to AOI members only. These stickers help safeguard the return of artwork.

Students and new illustrators

Our seminars and events, combined with the many services we offer, can provide practical support to illustrators in the early stages of their career.

Events

The AOI runs an annual programme of events which include one day seminars, evening lectures and thematic exhibitions. These include talks by leading illustrators as well as representatives from all areas of the illustration field, and cover such subjects as children's book illustration, aspects of professional practice, new technologies and illustrators' agents. AOI members are entitled to discounted tickets. To request further information or a membership application form please telephone +44 (0)20 7613 4328

Website

Visit our website at www.theAOI.com for details of the Association's activities, including samples from current and past journals, details of forthcoming events, the AOI's history and on-line portfolios.

Patrons
Glen Baxter
Peter Blake
Quentin Blake
Raymond Briggs
Chloe Cheese
Carolyn Gowdy
Brian Grimwood
John Hegarty
David Hughes
Shirley Hughes
Sue Huntley
Mick Inkpen
Donna Muir
Ian Pollock
Gary Powell
Tony Ross
Ronald Searle
Paul Slater
Ralph Steadman
Simon Stern
Peter Till
Janet Woolley

foreword

Michael Bramman

When I started as an illustrator there were illustration and graphics annuals but source books were not much in evidence. The accepted method for a prospective client to see your work was to arrange an appointment to show your portfolio. Despite the occasional frustrations and the time it took to achieve this, making personal contact was a valuable experience and I think still is for a new illustrator.

Now commissioners seem to have less time to devote to meetings with illustrators and many of the people we work with are scattered across the UK and abroad. This situation is redressed in part by the opportunity to listen and speak to commissioners at the seminars and events organised by the AOI. The calendar year ended with a one day forum on professional issues which attracted a capacity audience Communication through e-mail and web sites now give immediate access and source books have proliferated. Deciding which book to enter your work in that is most likely to result in assignments can give pause for thought.

The chances are that as you are reading this that choice has been made. Images 27 has exceeded all expectations with a record number of entries which has increased both the standard and variety of styles. A testament to the AOI's decision to continue to publish its own annual.

We are confident that the way the submissions are selected ensures the presentation of much of the best work produced in the UK, making it the obvious choice of commissioners.

With the exhibited work added to the AOI web site's expanding archive it becomes a lasting record of the year in illustration. This year we have again opted to commission Rachel Goslin, a graduate whose work also appears in the unpublished section to produce the cover and linking material.

The Images annuals are widely promoted and sold through major book retailers. While most are likely to be bought for reference or educational use hopefully some will also introduce illustration to a wider audience.

In joining The Creators Rights Alliance in March 2001 we aligned the AOI with other creative industries who share our objectives in preventing abuses of creators rights. As a united front we can lobby Parliament for changes in the law to combat restrictive practices. In the US The Graphic Artists Guild are pushing for a bill to be introduced which will cover these issues.

Despite the function of illustration as a visual means of communication the industry has been slow to raise its profile and increase public awareness. Public exhibitions of contemporary illustration are rare and the Images exhibition, and the V&A National Art Library Illustration Awards are among the few exceptions.

Illustration needs to be more proactive in looking for ways to align itself with social issues. An example of this approach was the New York Society of Illustrators memorial show the Prevailing Human Spirit following the disastrous events of September 11. Clearly that had world wide significance but anything that is of interest to the public could be responded to. Raising the awareness and interest in illustration arguably would create a demand which would be responded to by clients. Supply and demand would engender a more positive climate in which to push for increased fees.

The continuing quality of the Journal, the web site Discussion Board and the innovation of the Online Interview with Brian Grimwood as the first subject, and increased membership are all contributing factors to the progress the AOI has achieved over the past twelve months. Added to this list has to be the dedication of the staff, Council, Patrons, our publishing team and the volunteers who assist us on so many projects.

However we know there is no room for complacency and the work goes on. Watch this space.

Michael Bramman
AOI Chair

introduction

Angus Hyland

The first thing that came to mind when I was asked to write this introduction, was what an excellent title 'Images' is. On reflection, image maker sounds a more fitting job title than illustrator for some of the artists displayed in these pages. It is a great pity that a tabloid consuming public would misconstrue such a description as more befitting Max Clifford than Maxfield Parrish and yet most of the public are more familiar and (probably) more sympathetic to the work of illustrators than of the work of graphic designers. The youth of yesteryear, who were buying books of the Beatles lyrics illustrated by Alan Aldridge, are probably the kind of people who are now buying books such as Lucy Cousins' Maisy for their grandchildren.

Most people are probably aware of illustration long before they become aware of fine arts such as painting. I can plot my own aesthetic education from Picasso backwards via David Hockney, David Gentleman, Aubrey Beardsley, Arthur Rackham, whose illustrations for Kenneth Grahame's Wind in the Willows were something of a catalyst for me. An edition of that book fell on my lap as a child and was, as I remember it, the first book that I consciously enjoyed. However, how would I describe Rackham's role in my progress as a reader of books? Well, in my mind, he enabled me to enter a new world. The illustrations illuminated the narrative, opening a window to another dimension. In short, it kick-started my imagination. I think it may have led me deeper into the story than if I had been reading a book without illustrations.

Obviously, the combination of words and images is nothing new. Illustration has a history which stretches back way beyond Gutenberg (who for many was the first legitimate typographer) It is hard to imagine a medieval manuscript without the abundance of accompanying illustrations and ornamentation. Just as Rackham's illustrations brought Wind in the Willows to life for me, so the illuminated miniatures brought religious and secular texts to life, creating a visual language that was universal and, thus, transcended the barriers presented to many by the written word. The monastic scriptoria whose artists painstakingly illuminated manuscripts by candlelight are the true forebears of the modern illustrator.

All things considered, illustration has had rather a rocky journey over the last ten to fifteen years, and it's only quite recently that it has started to emerge from the wilderness. On the other hand, graphic design has flourished during the same period. No longer is it a subject relegated to relative obscurity. In terms of public recognition, the subject is now regarded as a serious career option. This was certainly not the case when I was an under graduate, when I would have to give my mother a list of 'pass notes' to help her explain exactly what it was her son was studying at art college. This was certainly never the case with friends of mine who studied illustration. I suppose their parents assumed that they would be creating the pictures for the next Rupert Bear annual. So why then did an art form so readily understood and adored become so marginalised as an adjunct to graphic design. Well, one crucial factor was of course the rise of the computer and, more specifically, the Apple Mac.

However, the Mac has also played an integral role in the illustration renaissance, and continues to do so. Certainly, the Mac played a dual role (both cause and effect) in the repositioning of the whole industry and, with this in mind, the dichotomy between the emerging digital and the traditional handcrafted illustrator became the premise for a book that I edited entitled Pen and Mouse: Commercial Art and Digital Illustration

(Laurence King Publishing, 2001). In recent years, design and other forms of visual communication have been more likely to create images using typography than illustration, which can often be too expensive and, in some cases can look rather dated. However, all that seems to be changing. More and more illustrators are looking to the wealth of technology that is now available. Often this leads to solutions that are entirely digital, whilst others work towards more balanced creations, where both technology and traditional methods are in evidence. In most cases, today's illustrators don't restrict themselves to "one trick", they are far more likely to carry portfolios that were compiled using pen, ink, gouache, laptop, magic markers, letterpress, laptops, scanners, digital cameras and the latest software packages. Illustrators are more aware than ever that the competition is intense, and that flexibility and versatility are just as important as raw talent.

The fruits of this renaissance are there for everybody to see. Current pop culture is awash with the work of illustrators and designer/illustrators. Illustration in its many guises has become more and more visible in everything from editorial design and fashion publicity, to advertising, music and television graphics. It is hard to imagine opening a broadsheet these days without discovering myriad examples of contemporary illustration, and it isn't just the fashion and lifestyle supplements either. The scene is blossoming and The British Council are supporting the cause to great effect. Picture This: Contemporary Illustration from London has so far visited venues as far and wide as Damascus and Tehran, and has recently completed a tour of Latin America (visiting venues in Caracas, Bogota and Santiago).

The Pentagram Award is awarded on an annual basis to illustrators represented in the

previous year's AOI Images annual. The winners are given the chance to exhibit their work in The Gallery at Pentagram and meet representatives from the design industry (and beyond) at a sponsored private view. Last year's exhibition reflected the wealth of talent and diversity currently on offer in an increasingly vibrant and inventive industry. The show was a great success, and introduced the work of Chris Kasch, Nick Hardcastle, Tom Gauld and Alex Williamson - not to mention the AOI - to an audience perhaps unaccustomed to exhibitions devoted solely to the world of contemporary illustration. Whilst the exhibition presented four completely different (yet equally accomplished) styles of illustration, it still represented only a fraction of what is currently on offer.

It is always incredibly difficult to choose such a small number of winners from the spectrum of talent on show in the Images annuals, and I expect this year's task to be no different. I would also like to take this opportunity to wish all of this year's contributors continued success and the very best of luck for the forthcoming future.

Angus Hyland
Partner, Pentagram

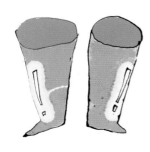

judges of images

Advertising

Francis Blake
Illustrator

Dr Leo De Freitas
Research Fellow/
Touring Exhibition Curator

Andy Myring
Design Director
Enterprise IG

Mary Claire Smith
Illustrator

Editorial

Colin Craig
Creative Director, 4c

Penny Garrett
Art Director
The Economist

Ivan Cottrell
Art Editor, Design Week

Steve May
Illustrator/Animator

Ryan Newey
Director, Fold 7

Martin Salisbury
Illustrator/Lecturer

Books

Neil Astley
Editor, Bloodaxe Books

Michelle Couston
Deputy Design Editor
Book Section
Sunday Times

Manisha Patel
Senior Design Manager/
Associate Art Director
Duncan Baird publishers

Simon Pemberton
Illustrator

Jonathan Williams
Illustrator

Children's Books

Jan Fearnley
Illustrator

Jemima Lumley
Art Director
Orchard Books

Caroline Sheldon
Literary Agent

Helen Stephens
Illustrator

New Media

Julia Bigham
V&A

Michael Branthwaite
Freelance Art Director

Shane Mc Gowan
Illustrator

Colin McHenry
Group Art Director
Centaur

Nigel Owen
Illustrator

Design

Kevin Hauff
Illustrator

Paul Hess
Illustrator

Stephen Petch
Art Director
Independent Magazine

Deborah Rae Smith
Hill Rae Smith Graphics

Student

Julia Coulson
Graphic Design Manager
John Lewis Partnership

Paul Davis
Illustrator

John Ellner
Colour House Graphics

Lucy Truman
Illustrator

Unpublished

Alison Eldred
Agent

Kathie Jenkins
European Illustration
Collection Hull

Lydia Monks
Illustrator

Graham Rawle
Artist/Illustrator

About the **illustrations**

M Medium
B Brief
C Commissioned by
F Firm

Awards

G Gold

S Silver

B Bronze

Advertising
Gold award winner

Ian Whadcock
G   23.00 Rome
M   Digital
B   Eastwing Volume 5
    promotional
    publishing based on
    Time and Location

G

C   Andrea Plummer
F   Eastwing

Jonathan Burton

B Hounded

M Model, photography, digital

B To illustrate a theatre poster advertising a play entitled 'Stranger in a Stranger Land'

B

C Anthony Seeley

F Mind The Gap Theatre Co.

Jill Calder
Campus Life

M Acrylic, ink

B Create an image encompassing as many elements of the Heriot-Watt University campus in Edinburgh which would appeal to young people considering their tertiary education options

C Kirsty Wilson
Karen Larter

F Heriot-Watt University

Jonathan Cusick
Guardian Rugby Coverage

M Acrylic

B Illustrate five rugby
manoeuvres in
a simple manner,
ending with 'Stopping
Joe Roff' (building
brick wall)

C Christine Saunders

F BMP DDB

Staffan Gnosspelius
Jazz Player

M Pencil

B Commissioned for the
cover of Henry's Jazz
Cellar's April-May
brochure, advertising
the club and the events
throughout Edinburgh

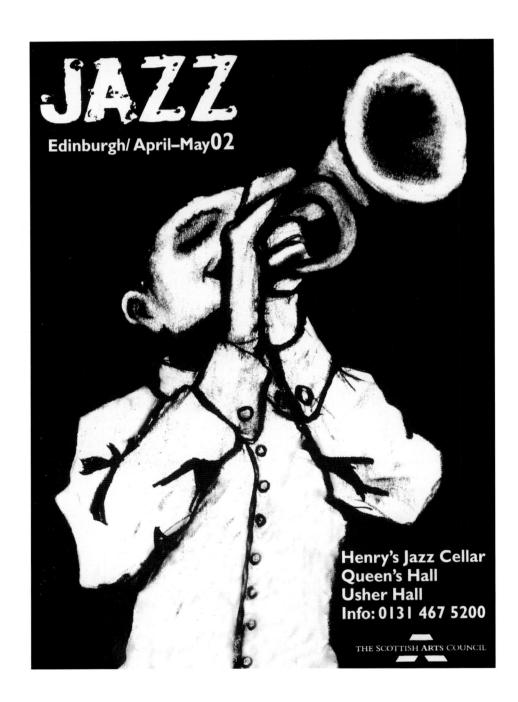

C Fiona Alexander

F Assembly Direct Limited

Helen Mills
Change for Change

M   Gouache

B   To illustrate an
interactive poster
to educate children
about fund raising
ideas (ladder and
boards are designed
to be filled in by
the children)

C   Juliet Blackledge

F   Christian Aid

Philip Nicholson
Tennis String

M Digital

B To illustrate in detail
the construction
of a tennis string

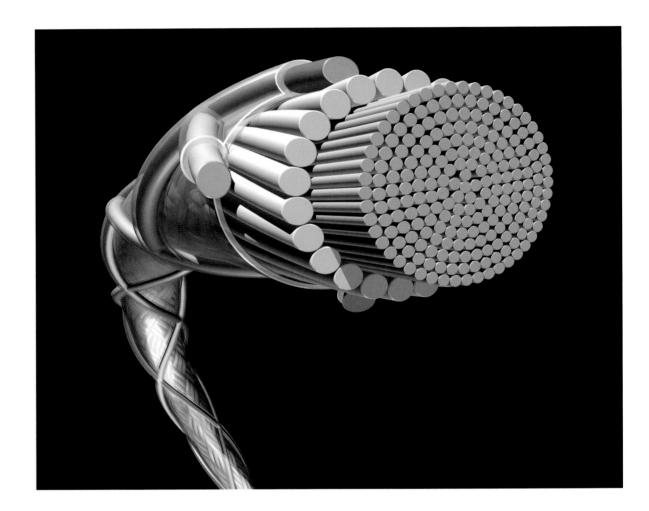

C Åse Inde

F Energy Project

Simon Pemberton

Youth Music – DJs   Youth Music – Folk

M   Mixed media

B   A series of posters
    for UK Youth Music
    Initiative to encourage
    0 – 18s into key
    music areas

F   Northbank Design

Maria Raymondsdotter

Scarf   TNT   Fire

M   Pen, ink and digital

B   To illustrate a series
    of ads for the Impulse
    deodorant campaign

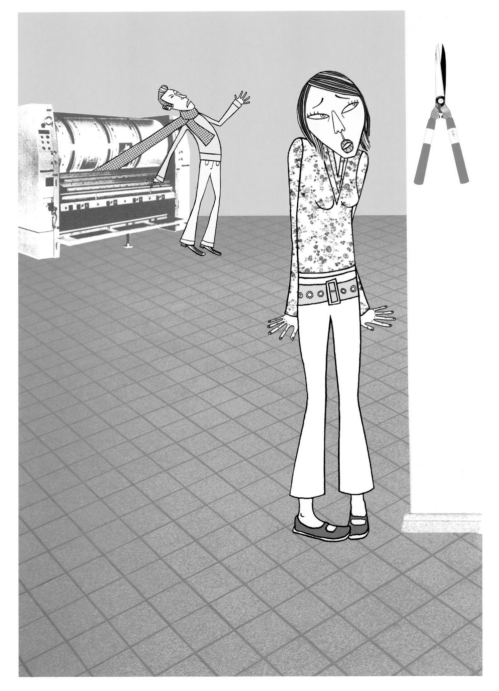

C   Tony McTear

F   BBH

Andy Smith

 S On Safari

M Original art, digital

B Produce an amusing
image with type,
to appear on the
Underground, with
a theme of Safari, to
promote London Zoo

S

F M&C Saatchi for
London Transport

Andy Smith
The Amazon

M Original art, digital

B Produce an amusing
   image with type,
   to appear on the
   Underground, with a
   theme of The Amazon
   that appeals to
   children, to promote
   Kew Gardens

Orange

M Original art, digital

B Produce an image
   with type promoting
   the letter B as a
   friendly letter

F M&C Saatchi for
   London Transport

F Lowe Lintas
   for Orange

Bob Venables

Adidas
Football Mutant

M Pencil, ink

B To produce a medical
drawing showing
a bonding of a new
football boot and
the foot

Martini Bianco

M Alkyd, acrylic

B To produce a poster
for Martini Bianco
reflecting a style of
Martini posters from
the 50s

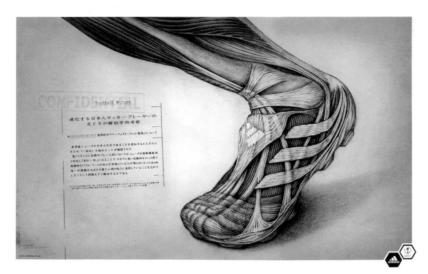

C Aya Kobayashi

F Saatchi / Saatchi
Tokyo

C Mark Reddy

F BMP DDB

Chris Watson
Bam-Boo
M Mixed media
B Flier for Ocean Rooms
   club, Brighton

Andy Watt
Virgin Mobile
M Mixed media
B One off campaign
   to coincide with
   V2002 festival
   for Virgin Mobile

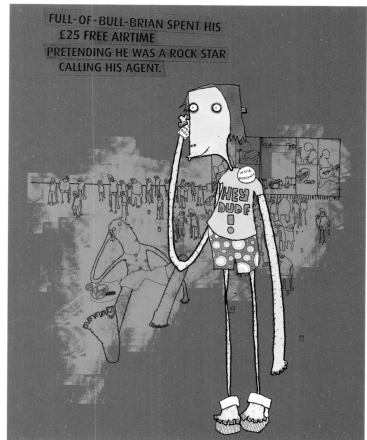

Neil Webb
Economy of Comfort

M Digital

B To illustrate
   concepts of comfort
   and economy for a
   leading hotel chain

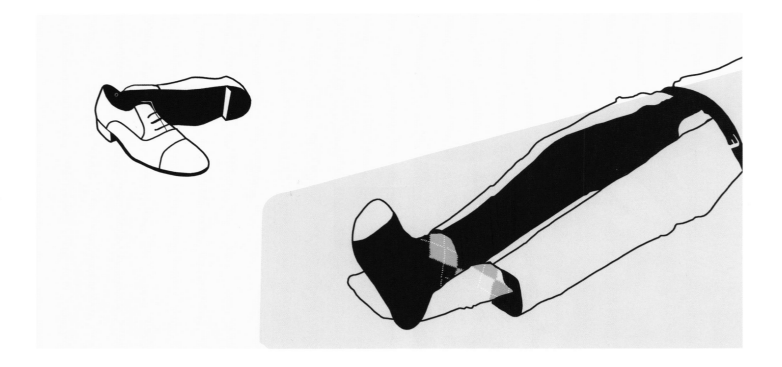

C Amber Casey
F BMP DDB Ltd

Design and new media
Gold award winner

Paul Wearing
G Quick Reference
for Counsellors
M Digital
B Brochure cover for
teachers/counsellors
guiding students
towards applying
to the University of
California, conveying
the ideas of mental
growth, student
diversity and vision

C Laura Cirolia
F University of California

Jonas Bergstrand
CAN.U.TLK
M Digital
B Depict the increasing
use of mobile internet
phones in Japan as a
means of conducting
market research

C David Freeman
F WPP
Atticus Journal

Paul Blow
Toxic Cotton

M Acrylic

B Fourteen illustrators
were asked to
customise reclaimed
wardrobes for an
ethical skate and bike
clothing company,
each illustrating an
environmental issue

C Phil Carter

F Carter Wong Tomlin

Michael Bramman
Hôtel Centre,
Entraygues

M   Acrylic

B   One of a series
of local scenes
for print collection

C   Nigel Atkins

F   Galerie du Don

Russell Cobb
Good Communication
(1/8)

M Acrylic

B 4 graphic stories for
BT's buyers' room
wall, illustrating
families teaching each
other important skills.
These link subtly to
the phones, eg. icing
the cake = texting

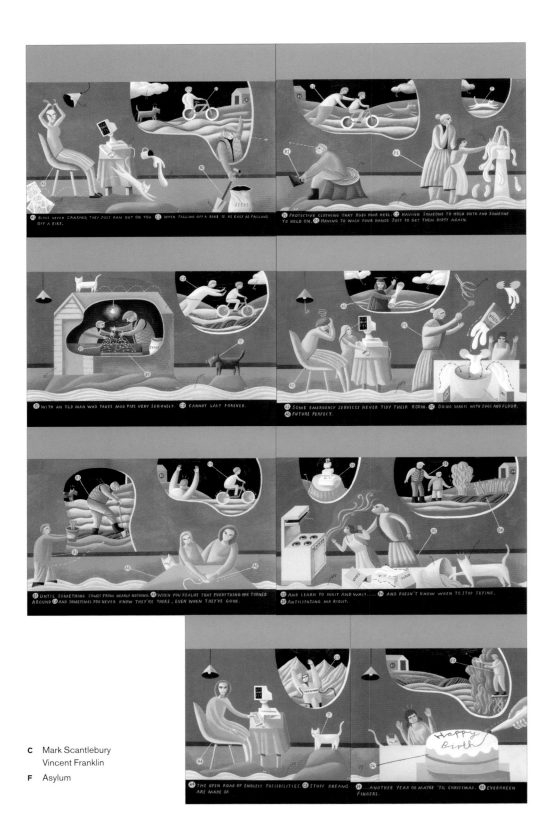

C Mark Scantlebury
Vincent Franklin

F Asylum

Our Journey

M Acrylic

B One of a series of
cards sent to Asylum
clients, illustrating
the companies core
values: listen, think,
create and solve

Izhar Cohen

Rudyard Kipling's
'Just So Stories'

M Pen, ink, watercolour

B On the occasion of
the centenary of the
'Just So Stories', the
brief was to illustrate
10 of the stories with
a focus on the animals
featured in each

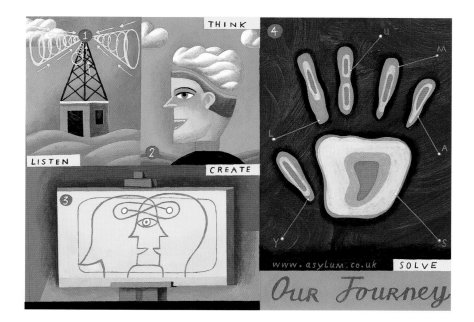

C Mark Scantlebury

F Asylum

C Jane Ryan

F Royal Mail

Cyrus Deboo
Slippers
M Digital
B Subscription card
for new media age
magazine 'Are you
Kitted Out for the
Interactive Economy?'

C Colin McHenry
F New Media Age

Ron Fuller
Circus

M Watercolour

B To produce a set
of images which
capture the energy
and imagination of
the circus

Jeff Fisher
Internet Brand
Relationships

M Acrylic

B Depict how
technology is bringing
a new level of
personalisation to
brand relationships

C Barry Robinson

F Royal Mail

C David Freeman

F WPP
Atticus Journal

Peter Grundy
Eyes
M Digital
B A series of banners
to illustrate the
various divisions of
the Ophthalmology
Society

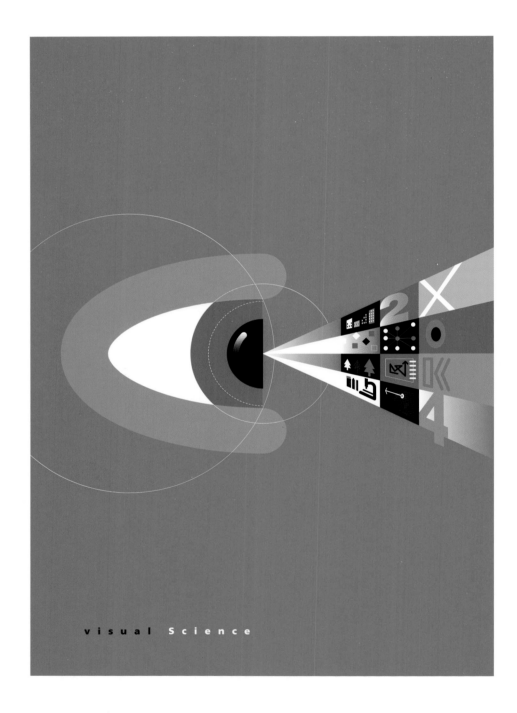

C Still Waters Run Deep
F Ophthalmology Institute

International **eye health**

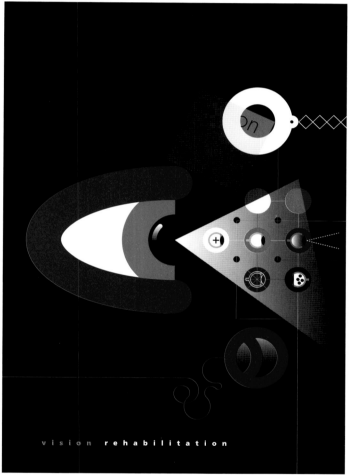

vision **rehabilitation**

George Hardie
Order by Number

M Silkscreen

B Image commissioned
by Trickett and Webb
for their Pizza To Go
calendar for
Augustus Martin

The Same Difference

M Pen and ink
separations

B Invited to produce
an image to be given
by Pentagram as
the company's
Christmas present
to the directors,
designers and staff

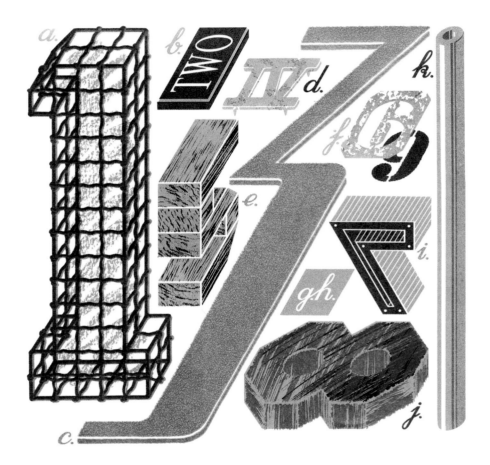

C Brian Webb
Lynn Trickett
Katja Thielen

F Trickett and Webb

C Angus Hyland

F Pentagram Design

Paul Hess
HSBC Funds
M Watercolour
B Brochure to
describe the variety
of 'hedge' funds
offered by HSBC

C Clive Morris
F Red Rocket

David Hitch

S Transport Guide:
Harrow

M Digital

B Transport for London
Guide to local areas
to show public
transport and
places of interest

S

C Mark Habis

F Spinner

Robert Hoare
Bushes

M Digital collage

B Produce a CD
   sleeve artwork for
   the Fatboy Slim remix
   of the Markus Nikolai
   track 'Bushes'

F Stylus

Frazer Hudson
A Journey

M   Digital

B   The illustration is to
be used as part of
a spreadsheet for
a series of seminars
around the theme of
"personal journeys",
featuring the highs and
lows along the way

C   Gayle Carpenter

F   Beyond Design

Have a Ball
This Xmas!

M Digital

B Produce a sequence
of humorous line
drawings which are
to be used within an
A6 flick book format
with the title 'Have a
Ball this Xmas'

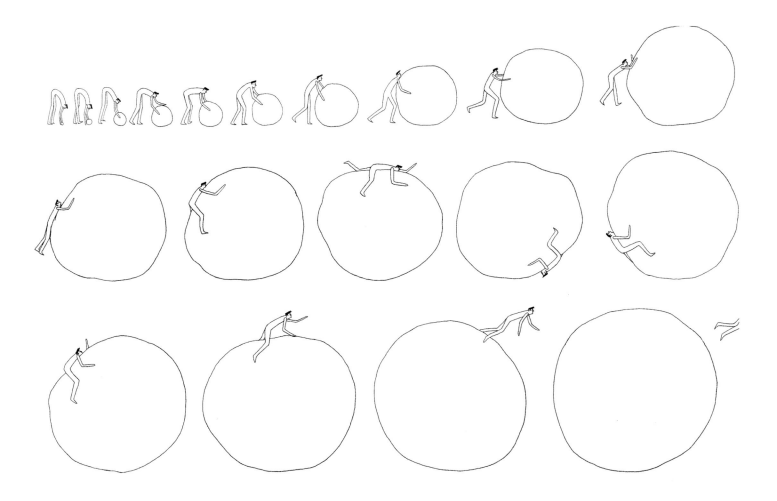

C Simon Robertson

F Identity Design

Jane Human
Coastlines - Royal
Mail presentation
stamp pack

M   Oil, graphite

B   To produce a series
of paintings and
drawings which
explore our interaction
with the British
coastline - designated
area from Berwick to
Scarborough

C   Philip Parker

F   Royal Mail Stamps

Per Karlen

We are all Unique

M Digital

B Interactive
CD-ROM: The project
communicates the
advantages of being
similar and the beauty
of being different. Two
twins take the viewer
through a voyage of
self-discovery

Our Mission

M Metallic colours
and black ink –
off white paper

B WPP Annual Report
and Accounts

Mick Marston
Atlantic Promotion

M Digital

B To produce a set
of coasters for
Atlantic Recordings
incorporating the
company logo
in each one

C Richard Bates

F Atlantic Records

Shane Mc Gowan
Never Look a Gift
Horse in the Mouth

M Digital

B Illustrate a common
idiom for inclusion
in agency brochure –
in this case 'Never
look a gift horse in
the mouth'

C Holly Veneble

F Three in a Box

Lydia Monks
Naughty but Nice
M Acrylic
B To design a set
of cards that
would appeal to
a young market

C Emily Holyfield
F The Art Group

Jai Moodie
Venus Postcard

M Pen, ink, G3 colour

B Produced for
promotional postcard
for Venus Flowers –
change of address
and new shop opening

C David Armstrong

F Venus Flowers

Tom Morgan-Jones

B www.snake-charmers.com

M Ink, digital

B Depict how the internet is being accepted into Indian culture

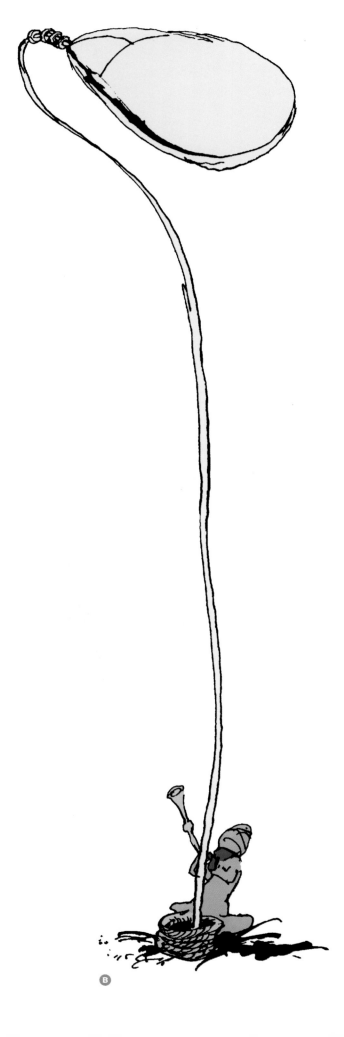

C David Freeman

F WPP
Atticus Journal

Tilly Northedge
The Life Cycle of an
Offshore Oil Field

M Digital

B Produce a diagram
showing the life
cycle of an offshore
oil field from
surveying, rig design,
manufacture and
installation through
to maintenance and
decommissioning

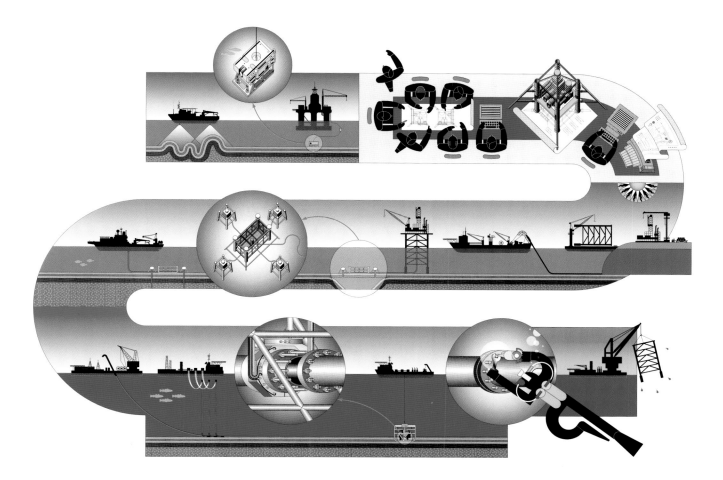

C Simon Shaw

F CGI Brandsense

Jackie Parsons
Collaboration
M Collage
B Depict a collaborative
consumer relationship
towards brands

Paul Powis
En Provence
M Oil on board
B To produce a black
and white atmospheric
image of a typical
French landscape for
a limited edition print

C David Freeman
F WPP
Atticus Journal

C Glyn Washington
F Washington Green

Nobby Sprouts
Energizer Batteries

M   Mixed media

B   Concept design
for TV commercial
showing a selection
of animals being
better equipped

C   Mario Cavalli

F   Aka Pizazz

James Tredray
Barclays University

M   Digital

B   To produce a series
of illustrations that
portray the relaxed,
modern atmosphere
at Barclay's University
centres. To be used as
graphics for interiors
and print material

Paul Wearing
Migraine
M Digital
B Produce illustration
for cover of brochure
about the nature
of migraine with
advice on combating
the symptoms of
the illness

Introducing
the University
M Digital
B Brochure cover
introducing UCAL
conveying it's diverse
cultural intake with the
idea that it will enable
students to embrace
and 'hold the world in
their hands'

Application for
Undergraduates
M Digital
B Brochure cover
conveying idea of a
diverse multi cultural
intake having the
possibilities in the
world opened to them
through education at
the University of
California

Answers for Transfers
M Digital
B Brochure cover
offering guidance
to students who want
to transfer to different
courses at the
University of California
conveying the ideas
of vision, direction
and student diversity

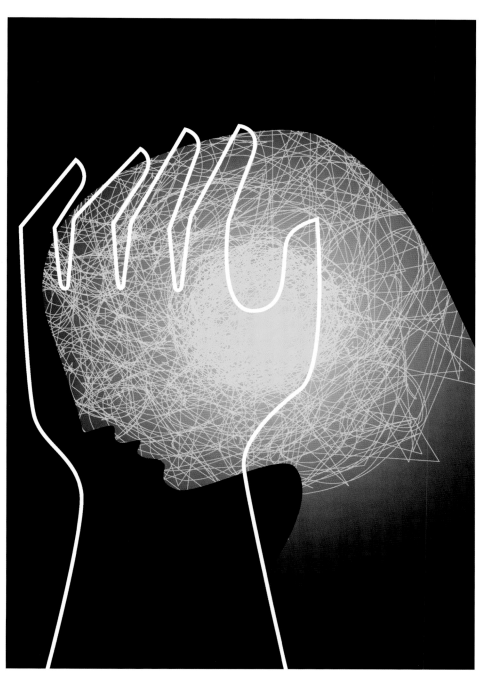

C Lucy Wise
F Forward

C Laura Cirolia
F University of California

Jonathan Williams
The Reading Room

M Digital

B A humorous
storyboard for
Benetton, showing
how a hi-tech
magazine room could
increase footfall
through a clothes store

C Tim Scott

F Haymarket Publishing

Editorial
Gold award winner

Andy Baker
 Frontiers – Cloning
M Digital
B To illustrate the
shadier side of
cloning technology
for the Radio Times
radio listings

G

C Sara Ramsbottom
F Radio Times

RadioTimes

Hashim Akib
Money Bags

M Acrylic

B Illustration for The
   Times for an article
   about investing as
   the tax year deadline
   draws near

C Martin Harrison

F The Times
   Money

A. Richard Allen

In the Dock

M Ink, digital

B An article examining
new legislation
protecting the rights
of animals (the so-
called 'Pets' Charter')

'Top Pocket' Relationships

M Ink, digital

B An article describing
'Top Pocket'
relationships: causal
sexual relationships
between two single
friends, a mutually
convenient
arrangement with
no commitment

C Ben Brannan

F The Guardian

Andy Baker

The Data Collector

M Digital

B A feature story about
new data encryption
methods. A data key
can now be swiped
from the airwaves

Who Owns
the Genome?

M Digital

B A feature story about
the ownership of
discoveries in the
field of gene theory

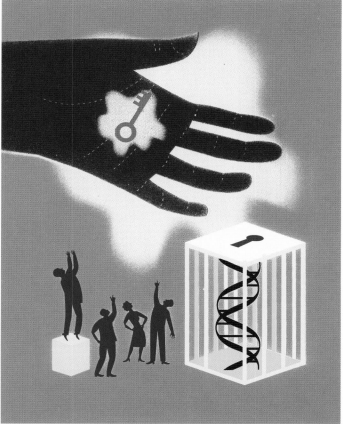

C Alison Lawn

F New Scientist

Paul Blow
The Routes of English

M Paint, digital

B Tracing the many
routes of English.
Programme One
specialised in North
America and the rise
of Hispanic English
in Spanish Harlem

C Sara Ramsbottom

F Radio Times

RadioTimes

Stuart Briers
Brain Coral

M Digital

B To create an image
to accompany
the winning poem
in a natural history
competition run by
a national magazine

C Simon Bishop

F BBC Wildlife

Nigel Buchanan
Why Can't a Woman
be More Like a Man
M Gouache
B A comedy about
female desire,
Viagra and the
pharmaceutical
industry

Jonathan Burton
Under Pressure
M Drawing
B Illustrate
magazine article

C Sara Ramsbottom
F Radio Times

C Gary Cook
F FT Business Magazine

RadioTimes

Jill Calder
Bad Back?

M Digital

B Response to an
   article by an osteopath
   which explained
   that most back pain
   was caused by the
   lower spine and pelvis
   being misaligned

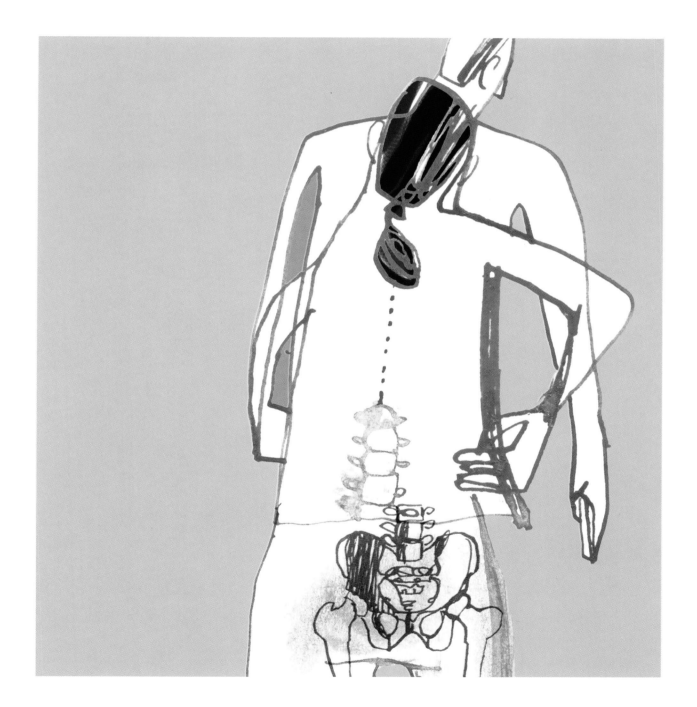

C Jane Wright

F The Sunday Herald

Jill Calder
Feet First

M Digital

B An article about
reflexology, in
particular how it
could help stress
headaches and
related eye strain

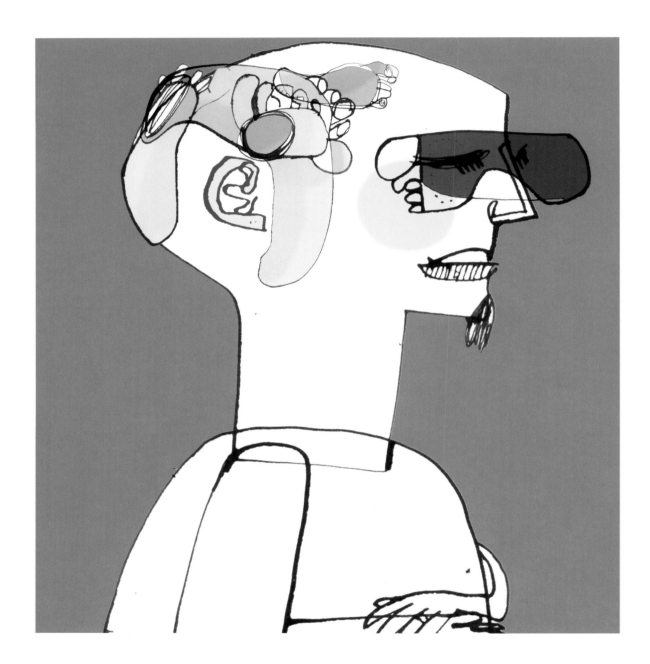

C Jane Wright

F The Sunday Herald

Russell Cobb
Are you Imploding?

M   Acrylic

B   To illustrate a feature
about working from
home showing the
pitfalls that arise
during the day.
The article asks the
question: Are you
imploding?

C   Darren Long

F   John Brown
Citrus Publishing

Miles Cole
Music Industry Monster

M Collage, digital

B Aggressive
anti-pirate policies
by music industry
giants detrimental
to AppleMac users

C James Walker

F Macworld

Sarah Coleman
Deadly Poisonous
M Drawing, digital
B Illustrate different
toxic and non-toxic
funghi, without
looking like a dry
text book diagram

C Perry Cleveland-Peck
F EMAP Active

Matthew Cook

Montepulciano

M Acrylic, inks

B The illustrator was
flown to Tuscany
for three days, to
follow in the author's
footsteps, recording
certain preselected
locations, other
personal sketches
were also chosen

The Wye Valley

M Acrylic, inks

B The opening
Illustration (front page)
of a six week series
tracing interesting
areas of the British
countryside, showing
the diverse characters
of each area

C Martin Harrison

F The Times
Travel

Jonathan Cusick
Lester Piggott

M Acrylic

B A caricature of the
jockey in my style
but suggesting an
old cigarette card for
'My Sporting Hero'
feature

C Tracey Gardiner

F Radio Times

RadioTimes

Cyrus Deboo

Specialist
Restructuring Services

M Digital

B Illustrate the growth
of specialist
restructuring services

www dot

M Digital

B Cover illustration for
supplement about
e-commerce websites.
Customers want
websites that are
easy to use and do
not induce a migraine

C Rachel James

F Middle Market

C Colin McHenry

F Precision Marketing

Rowena Dugdale
Junk Bonds

M Mixed media

B To illustrate the
risks of investing
in junk bonds

Jonathan Edwards
Alvaro Siza

M Pen, ink, digital

B A portrait of eminent
Portuguese architect
to accompany an
interview. The portrait
was also to reflect the
style of his architecture

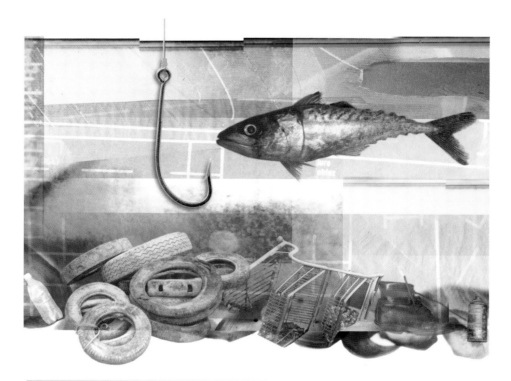

C Ingrid Shields

F Investors Chronicle

C Stuart Ratcliffe

F World Architecture

**Fine & Dandy
(Mick Marston
v. Pat Walker)**
Mac Gaming

M Digital

B Editorial piece for
MacUser magazine
for article on games
for the Mac

C Jason Simmons

F MacUser

Simon Farr
Chris Tarrant

M Pen, ink, watercolour

B Caricature of
Chris Tarrant,
TV personality

C Geoffrey Powell

F TV Times

Jason Ford
Caller Waiting

M   Acrylic, ink

B   Animated menacing
    shadows stealing a
    mobile phone from
    a youth without him
    noticing to illustrate
    the sudden increase
    in this particular crime

C   Martin Harrison

F   The Times
    Money

Andrew Foster
Digital Song Bird
M   Mixed media
B   To communicate
the ease of buying
music and sound
effects online

C   Sarah Watson
F   Shots Magazine

Andrew Foster
Construction
Manager Stress,
'Under Pressure'

M   Mixed media

B   To communicate
management stress
in the building
industry for the front
cover and inside
double page spread

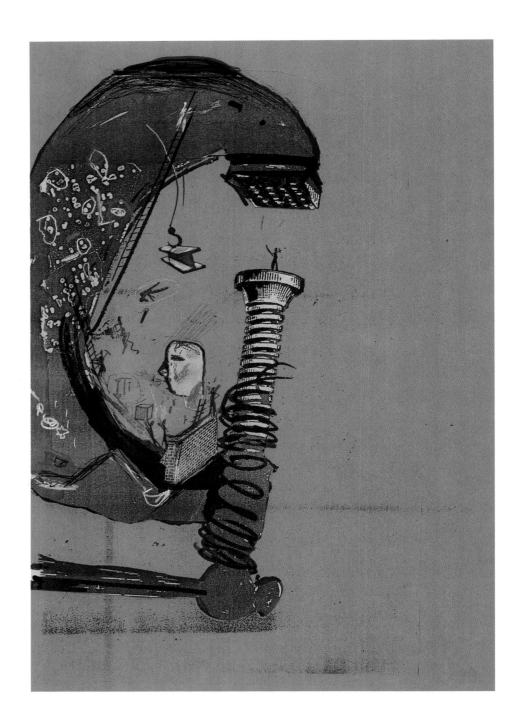

C   Richard Krzyzak

F   Construction Manager
The Builder Group

James Fryer

The Houses that
Saved the World

M Acrylic

B To illustrate how
soaring house prices
have helped save
certain economies
around the world –
front cover illustration

Present at
the Creation

M Acrylic

B Cover illustration for
a survey of America –
America has both
the chance and
the motivation to
reshape the world

Who'll Stoke
the Boiler?

M Acrylic

B To illustrate the
reducing of principal
teachers within
schools and the effect
this will have on
certain subjects

Double Vision

M Acrylic

B To illustrate the
benefits of being
able to run 2
monitors from 1 PC

Sheriff for the World

M Acrylic

B Inside illustration
for a survey of
America – the attacks
of September 11th
have given America a
powerful new motive
for global activism

Which Way Now?

M Acrylic

B The European Union
has come a long way
since its introduction,
but which way does it
go now?

C Graeme James

F The Economist

C Una Corrigan

F The Economist

C Steve Place

F The Scottish
Times Educational
Supplement

C Hazel Bennington

F PC Magazine

C Una Corrigan

F The Economist

C Susan Buchanan

F Worldlink Magazine

James Fryer

The Fightback
Against Globalisation

M Acrylic

B To illustrate the
fight back against
globalisation – smaller
companies now being
able to take on larger
corporations

The New Empire

M Acrylic

B To illustrate America
as the new Roman
Empire – no nation
since Rome has
loomed so large
above the others

Geoff Grandfield

One Night in Winter

M Chalk, pastel

B Thriller drama set at
Christmas in Beth's
hostel, but when two
strangers arrive the
festivities take on
a different meaning

C Susan Buchanan

F Worldlink Magazine

C Sue Vago

F The Economist

C Sara Ramsbottom

F Radio Times

Jo Hassall
Wishing Carefully
M Mixed media
B To illustrate a
piece of fiction
by Marian Keyes

F Express Newspapers

Matt Herring

Jamaica

M   Digital, collage

B   To embrace the
    vibrancy of Jamaican
    music, culture and
    life as TV celebrates
    the 40th anniversary
    of the island's
    independence

Paul Hess

Escape and Explore

M   Watercolour

B   Supplement cover
    to illustrate weekend
    breaks for couples,
    exploring cities
    and the countryside,
    where to stay and eat

C   Vicky Smart

F   Radio Times

C   Sharron Morgan

F   Times Weekend

Robin Heighway-Bury
Baby Blues
M   Digital
B   Article on post
    natal depression

C   Martin Colyer /
    Hugh Kyle
F   Reader's Digest

Fiona Hewitt

Daylight Robbery

M Digital

B The illustration is about retail theft as a constant problem for security managers, and how they could use offenders' perspectives to build up strategies to guard against theft, using research from The Searman Centre

E-Community

M Digital

B A new type of information management system will unite landlords and tenants in cyberspace

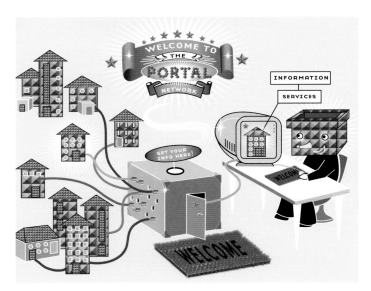

C Simona Cooke
F SMT
The Builder Group

C Richard Krzyzak
F Property Week
The Builder Group

Tobias Hickey
Cooling and Ventilation

M Digital

B The design of
an effective air
conditioning system
within buildings

David Hitch
Flash Money

M Digital

B Icons to illustrate
the various financial
options open
to retired people

C Jason Harris

F Building Services Journal
The Builder Group

C Lori Goudie

F Modern Maturity Magazine

David Humphries
Hello Sailor

M   Digital, collage

B   To use the author's
    portrait in a collage
    about her dislike
    of boats

C   Graham Black

F   FT

New England

M Digital, collage

B To illustrate a travel article about Valentine's Day in New England, an unseasonal but beautiful time to visit the area

Desks

M Digital, collage

B To depict how a person's generosity and personality is related to the tidiness of their desk

C Graham Black

F FT

C Darren Long

F Alodis Magazine

Rod Hunt
The Pitfalls of
Lingerie Shopping

M Digital

B Illustrate a lingerie
department and
some of the people
that frequent it

C Damian Wilkinson

F Maxim

Itchy Animation
Little Nellie

M   Digital

B   To create a highly
realistic, detailed and
accurate rendering
of a vehicle from
a James Bond film

Marie Hélène Jeeves
Get Set for E – Day

M   Pen, ink

B   To represent the
nations of Europe
coping with the
introduction of
the Euro

C   Steve Scanlan

F   GE Fabbri

C   Martin Colyer

F   Reader's Digest

Adrian Johnson

Bingham

M Digital

B Regular, weekly
illustration slot
tackling legal issues.
This example dealt
with incompetence
in arbitration. Fun,
amusing and eloquent

Having the Builders in

M Mixed media

B To illustrate an
article on 'Having
the Builders In'

C Sam Jenkins

F Building
The Builder Group

C Bruno Haward

F The Guardian

Satoshi Kambayashi
Internet Security
M Digital
B The internet users
are not fully aware
of the security issues

C Dana Mansfield
F New Law Journal

Chris Kasch
The Waiter

M   Acrylic

B   To illustrate multi-
    angled views of
    a frozen moment
    in a restaurant,
    ranging from large
    overviews to the
    smallest detail

C   Martin Harrison
    Pryderi Gruffydd

F   Times Newspapers
    Limited Marketing

Elisabeth Lecourt
Stocking Ladders
M   Collage, pencil
B   To illustrate an article
    based on the ladders
    from the Bibliothèque
    National de Paris

C   Malgosia Szemberg
F   World of Interiors

Matt Lee
Use Your Imagination!

M   Mixed media

B   From a story about
how a daydreaming
school boy found that
the process of writing
helped his imagination
– the TES Write Away
literary competition

Henning Löhlein
Spring Cleaning

M   Acrylic

B   Sometimes the spring
cleaning can be a
rather difficult job,
especially after the
builders have been in

C   Trevor Wilson

F   TES

Nick Lowndes

Snaring the
Corrupters

M Print

B This piece was
about keeping pace
with and cracking
down on corrupt
business practices,
and how you manage
those international
business trades

Leonie Lord

Imagination
Without Chains

M Pen, ink, digital

B Surrealism – an
evening of debate
and music live from
the Tate Modern

C Simona Cooke

F SMT
The Builder Group

C Sara Ramsbottom

F Radio Times

RadioTimes

David Lyttleton
Going it Alone
M   Digital
B   An illustration to
    accompany an
    interview with
    Benedetta Tagliabue

James Marsh
The Borrowed Eye
M   Acrylic on canvas
B   To illustrate article
    about how the eye
    has not changed
    throughout evolution

C   Stuart Ratcliffe
F   World Architecture
    The Builder Group

C   Tom Rosinski
F   Natural History
    Magazine USA

Jan Martin
Manhandled?

M Collage

B Women in publishing:
are men still the ones
in control or are
women breaking
through the glass
ceiling?

C Melanie Ashby

F Mslexia Publications

Richard May
Yojimbo

M Digital

B Depict the Ronin
character from
Kurosawa's 1961
film 'Yojimbo'
(The Bodyguard) to
accompany a review

Steve May
Trustworthy

M Digital

B Microsoft, supplement
illustration about being
secure on the internet

C Michael Booth

F Time Out London

C Rachel James

F Caspian Publishing

John McFaul

How to Prevent Choking

M Digital

B A rather witty article
surrounding the
subject of the
prevention of choking

Pop!

M Digital

B Are home prices
too high and
about to undergo
a major pop!?

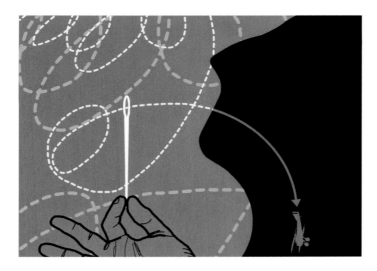

C Maggie Murphy

F The Guardian

C David McKenna

F Money Mail

Belle Mellor

B Crystal Clear

M Pen and ink, digital

B For an article
reviewing a book
by David Crystal,
explaining the
meaning of lost
and obscure words

Bad Boss

M Pen and ink

B Bosses who bully
the office staff

Swallow This

M Pen and ink, digital

B For an article on the
ethics of neuroscience
and the future of mood
altering medication

C Nick Robins

F Shakespeare's Globe

C Carol Young

F James Ireland Design

C Una Corrigan

F The Economist

Toronto Sings
the Blues
M Pen and ink
B To illustrate an article
named 'Toronto Sings
the Blues' about the
down turn in the city's
fortunes

Homeless
M Pen and ink
B For an article on the
housing situation in
Toronto where the gap
between the haves and
have nots is growing

Smile!
M Pen and ink, digital
B The ethics of
neuroscience and
the future of mood
altering medication

C Shelley Frayer
F University of Toronto
Magazine

C Shelley Frayer
F University of Toronto
Magazine

C Una Corrigan
F The Economist

Kate Miller

The Perfect Candidate

M Digital

B To illustrate the
perfect candidate
and what you have to
do in an increasingly
competitive job market
to get that dream job

Mark Oldroyd

The Haunting

M Acrylic

B 19th century ghost
story – Alexander
finds himself taken
over by an unseen
presence and begins
to act out of character

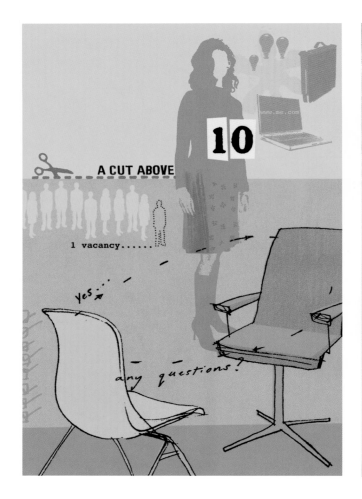

C Caroline Roberts

F Graphics International

C Sara Ramsbottom

F Radio Times

RadioTimes

Gunnlaug Moen Hembery
The Bad Things
About Celebrity Life

M Pen, ink, digital

B Article about when
the author experiences
the horror of fame and
the expectations of
photographers and
journalists of glamour
and fashion magazines

Dettmer Otto
Manhattan

M Digital

B Essay: three weeks
after the attack on
the WTC the author
reflects on the initial
terrified response
and the effects for
the future

Paquebot
Taming of Globalisation

M Digital

B Liberal market
economy turns
the quest for profit
into an engine of
social progress

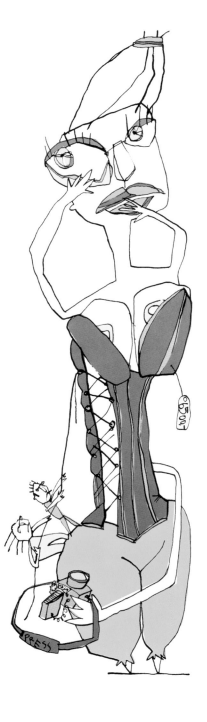

C Gudleiv Forr

F Dagbladet

C Steve Petch

F The Saturday
Independent
Magazine

C Una Corrigan

F The Economist

Steve Parkes
Instant Hospital

M Digital

B To create a fictitious
product using the
idea of an instant
hospital to convey
the throwaway nature
of the schemes

Simon Pemberton
Walking a Tightrope

M Mixed media

B To show the
precarious nature
of publishing
'Heavyweight'
Reader's Digest
finances and their
purchase of a much
smaller company
to carry them out
of danger

Broadband Internet

M Mixed media

B Cover image
comparing new high
speed broadband
internet access
to the previous slow
speed access

C Sam Jenkins

F Building
The Builder Group

F Folio (USA)

F The Guardian

Beverly Philps
Secret Agents

M   Digital

B   A behind the scenes
deal to promote unity
between surveyors
and estate agents

C   Colin Williams

F   Property Week
The Builder Group

Ian Pollock
Prince Philip

M Watercolour, ink

B Portrait of
Prince Philip

C Maggie Murphy
F The Guardian Weekend

Shonagh Rae
Unsung Heroes

M   Digital

B   Cover for relaunch
issue to show the
stress, fear and
pressure housing
officers confront
every day

C   Richard Krzyzak

F   Housing Today
The Builder Group

Darren Raven

Snakes and Ladders

M Digital

B To convey the ups
and downs of
architects' salaries
using the analogy of
snakes and ladders

Wild Wadi Aqua Park

M Digital

B The wild Wadi Aqua
park in Dubai at the
Jumeirah Beach resort

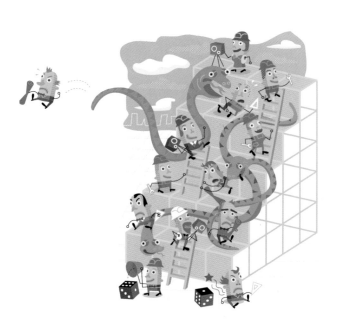

C Sam Jenkins

F Building
The Builder Group

C Jason Harris

F Building Services
Journal
The Builder Group

Matthew Richardson

Male Hormones   Female Hormones

M Mixed media

B Two from a series
of illustrations for
an article exploring
hormones and the role
they play in making us
the people we are

C Wayne Ford

F Observer Magazine

David Rooney

Afghan Stories No.1	Afghan Stories No.2	Afghan Stories No.3
M Scraperboard	**M** Scraperboard	**M** Scraperboard
B Illustrate true stories told by Afghan children about life under the Taliban regime. A young boy flouts kite flying ban	**B** A young girl aids father in selling baby brother	**B** A young girl steals a news reporter's pen and note pad

C Lawrence Bogle

F Times Supplement Ltd

Brett Ryder
Scoop

M   Digital

B   To portray project
    members and in-team
    insurance brokers
    as trapeze artists
    whose safety net is
    held by the insurer

C   Sam Jenkins

F   Building
    The Builder Group

Paul Slater

At Home
with the Snails
M Acrylic
B A comedy play, in
which Alex's parents
fake their deaths,
leading to him finding
solace in his obsession
about snails

Untitled 2
M Acrylic
B A striking illustration
for the front cover
of the Christmas
Radio Times using
'Christmas trees'
as a theme

Untitled 1
M Acrylic
B Caricature of
Melvyn Bragg as
'God of the Arts'
surrounded by some
of his favourite guests

It was not to be
M Acrylic
B An article by comedian
Tony Hawks about
A-level students being
set the wrong exam

C Sara Ramsbottom
F Radio Times

C Shem Law
F Radio Times

C Laura Hall
F Radio Times

C Martin Colyer
F Reader's Digest

RadioTimes

RadioTimes

RadioTimes

Jason Stavrou

Drop Some Acid

M Mixed media

B Editorial piece for
Men's Health
magazine to illustrate
a man suffering from
acid-reflux disease

Mad World

M Mixed media

B Editorial piece for the
Big Issue, to illustrate
a short humorous
story on large
Norwegian penguins

C Amanda Scope

F Men's Health
Magazine

C Micheal Branthwaite

F Big Issue Magazine

David Tazzyman
Clerkenwell Guide

M Original art, digital

B Produce an
image for the
2002 Clerkenwell
Festival – show
people meeting
and socialising
at the festival

F The Guardian for The
Clerkenwell 'Guide'

Michelle Thompson
Sky

M   Collage

B   Illustration about
The Friends of the
Earth's achievements
in the last 10 years
for Earthmatters
Magazine

C   Sarah Denney

F   Friends of the Earth

Nancy Tolford
Gold Beauty

M Digital

B A review of beauty
products made with
gold for the holiday
party season

C Graham Ball
F The Times Magazine

Paul Wearing
Future Medicine

M Digital

B Having mapped the
human genome, the
race is on for biotech
companies to make
the breakthrough in
understanding protein
construction with high
power computers

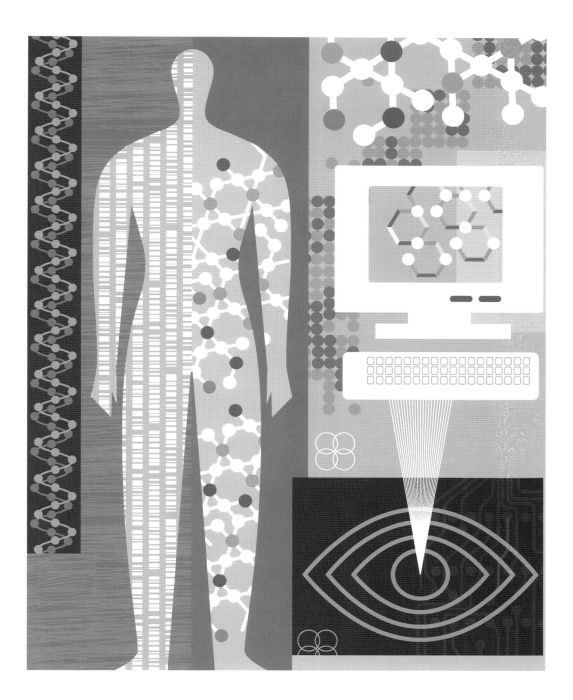

C Gretchen Smelter

F Smart Money

Paul Wearing
Tamoxifen

M Digital

B Illustrate feature
about the history of
the drug Tamoxifen
and its acceptance by
cancer specialists in
the targeted treatment
of breast tumours

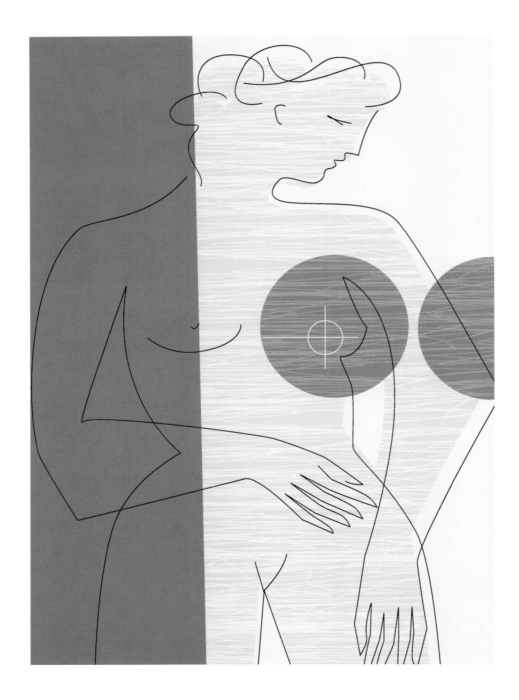

C Gary Cochran

F Telegraph on
Saturday Magazine

Louise Weir
The Renaissance
of Italian Design

M Acrylic

B Produced for a
Blueprint cover
on the renaissance
of Italian design

Ian Whadcock
His and Hers DIY
M Digital
B Feature on the stress
and strains of DIY
with your partner over
matters of taste in
terms of decoration

C Bruno Haward
F Weekend Guardian

Corporate Relocation

M Digital

B To illustrate the fluid market in corporate office space in the European Union

S Scrap the CAP

M Digital

B Article about the failings of Europe's common agricultural policy

Hitting the Jackpot

M Digital

B How to crack the worlds great unsolved mathematical problems. Highlighting the enormous prize money on offer to those providing successful solutions

C Martin Dixon

F Plan Magazine

C Martin Colyer
Hugh Kyle

F Reader's Digest

C Colin Brewster

F New Scientist
Reed Business Information

Jonathan Williams

Godless in the
Garden of Eden

M Digital

B Since the beginning
of creation we've been
experts at deceiving
ourselves and each
other. Fay Weldon
explains why lies
appear more palatable
than the truth

Princess Caucubu
goes Shopping

M Digital

B A short story by
Roberto Uria looks at
the vagaries of Cuban
society through the
minutiae of street life

C Denny Barnes

F Good Housekeeping

C Vanessa Baird

F New Internationalist

Sharon Williams
Blount Rise

M Acrylic

B Create a mysterious
magical character
disguised as an
ordinary eccentric
neighbour for this
short story

C Jane Stone

F IPC Magazines

Lee Woodgate
Future City
M Digital
B To produce an image
   reflecting the 'future'
   to be used as the
   contents DPS for
   MacUser magazine
   allowing ample space
   for all typo

C Jason Simmons
F MacUser

Children's books
Gold award winner

Jan Fearnley
G Mr Wolf and the
Three Bears 1
M Ink, watercolour
B 'Save me a big piece,'
(Grandma said)
'...a very big piece.
I'm starving!'

C Lisa Kershaw
F Egmont Books Ltd

Jamel Akib
The Pit and
the Pendulum

M   Chalk pastel

B   Create a cover 'The
Pit and the Pendulum'
specifically for a
younger readership

C   Shiree Nathoo

F   Nathoo Design for
Heinemann Books

Simon Bartram
Man on the Moon
(A Day in the Life of Bob)

M Acrylic

B A picture book
written and illustrated
by the artist about
the life of Bob, the
man on the moon and
his experiences with
tourists and aliens

Jan Fearnley
Mr Wolf and the
Three Bears 2

M Ink, watercolour

B For Baby Bear's
dish, they looked in
the big recipe book.
Soon they found the
perfect thing to make.
A birthday cake!

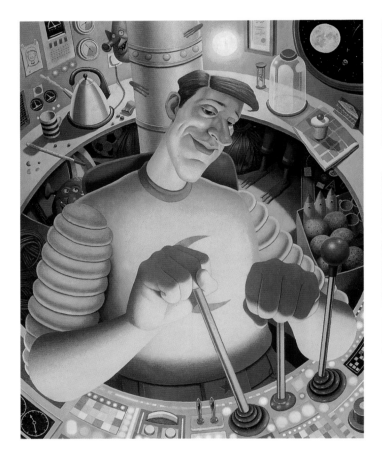

C Mike Jolley

F Templar Publishing

C Lisa Kershaw

F Egmont Books Ltd

Madeleine Floyd
Captain

M   Mixed media
B   Illustration for the
    forthcoming book
    by Madeleine Floyd
    entitled 'Captain's Purr'

C   Judith Elliott
F   Orion Publishing

Cathy Gale

Frankenstella 1,4,5

M Gouache, collage

B Stella warns mother
of monster lurking
in video shop, then
embarks on wild
chase across
B-movie country

C Sarah Odedina

F Bloomsbury

Richard Johnson

	I Want Roast Chicken!		The Hen House
M	Acrylic	**M**	Acrylic
B	The children's story 'Don't Cry Sly' – Sly's mother is hungry, she wants chicken!	**B**	Another scene from the story, illustrating Little Red's house and Sly's den

C Misuti Chatterji

F Mantra Publishing

Simone Lia
Follow the Line

M Gouache

B 'Is this the moon?'
Bruce asked a
strange looking bird.
'No, it's a snowy
mountain,' said the bird

C Phil Powell

F Egmont Books Ltd

Mark Marshall
Stop, Elephant, Stop!

M Acrylic

B A story about jungle
animals trying to keep
cool in the sun by
jumping in a water hole

C Paula Burgess

F Gullane
Children's Books

Sarah Mc Menemy
The Puppy Found a
Wastepaper Basket

He Thought Rosie
Looked Funny

M Collage, gouache

B To develop a story
as a pre-school
picture book around
a dog image

C Denise Johnston-Burt

F Walker Books

Lydia Monks

B My Cat's Weird

M Mixed media

B This is a scene where a little boy's cat has flown him away in a home-made aeroplane to visit his exotic cat cousins

B

C Ramona Reihill

F Egmont Books

Mary Murphy
Koala

M Digital

B 'Where do flowers
come from?' she asks.
Badger and Racoon
are sure they know

C Phil Powell

F Egmont Books Ltd

Nathan Reed
Toby's Favourite
Flying Ride

M Acrylic

B Image produced for
children's picture book
'Toby's Funfair Fish'

Lucy Richards
Night Monkey,
Day Monkey

M Acrylic

B 'Stop!' said Night
Monkey. 'Screeching
owls, the colour of
peas and carrots!'
Day Monkey laughed
and said, 'Don't be
daft, haven't you
heard of parrots?'

C Chris Inns

F Puffin

C Suzanne Cocks

F Egmont Books Ltd

Helen Stephens

 Poochie-Poo 1   Poochie-Poo 2

M Acrylic

B I wrote and illustrated
a picture book about
Butch who is... well...
butch! And Victor who
is... erm... not so butch

C Maria O'Neill
Designer: Ness Wood

F David Fickling Books

Marsha White
Some Goats
Love Gardening
M Collage, acrylic
B A spread from
a self-written
children's book
'Goats are Good!'
for Tango Books

C Sheri Safran
F Tango Books

Bee Willey
Bob Robber
and Dancing Jane

M Mixed media

B To illustrate the
finale of the love story
between Bob and
Jane – Bob coming
out of the darkness
and dancing with her
into the sun rise

C Ian Craig

F Random
Children's Books

Books
Gold award winner

Jason Ford

G The Heart
   of the Matter
M Gouache
B Audio cassette
   sleeve cover
   image of Graham
   Greene's novel

G

C Matt Bookman
F BBC Radio Collection

Ivan Allen

B Paul Temple and
the Geneva Mystery

M Digital

B Compact disc sleeve
cover image of
Francis Durbridge's
famous BBC Radio
detective character

B

C Matt Bookman

F BBC Radio Collection

BBC Audiobooks

Russell Cobb

The Great United
Bumper McBurger

M Acrylic

B Design a cover
incorporating a
map of the American
states for Peter
Biddlecombe's travels
around America

Brigid Collins

Samurai William

M Mixed media, collage

B Book cover for
a Giles Milton
book on the first
Englishman to open
trade negotiations
in Japan. For
Hodder & Stoughton

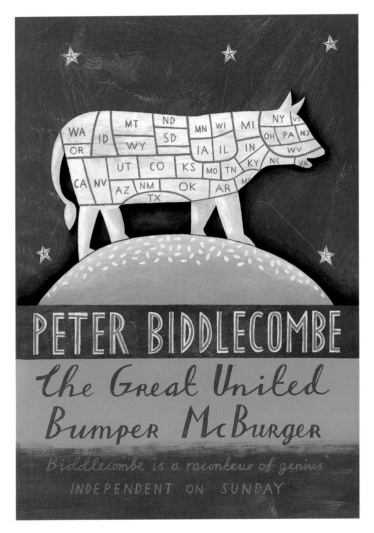

C Duncan Spilling

F Time Warner Books UK

C Ian Hughes

F Mousemat Design

Nicky Cooney
Puddings in a Panic
M Pen and ink
B A cookery book
of quick and
simple puddings

C Judith Robertson
F R+R for Colt Books

Chris Corr

S A Suitable Boy

M Gouache

B Audio cassette
sleeve cover image
of Vikram Seth's novel

S

C Matt Bookman

F BBC Radio Collection

BBC Audiobooks

Mark Hudson

The Fellowship
of the Ring

M Digital

B Compact disc sleeve
cover images for the
three books in J.R.R.
Tolkien's epic trilogy,
The Lord of the Rings

The Two Towers

The Return of the King

Mowgli Stories

M Digital

B Audio cassette
sleeve for Rudyard Kipling's
Jungle Book short stories

C Matt Bookman

F BBC Radio Collection

BBC Audiobooks

C Matt Bookman

F BBC Cover to Cover

BBC Audiobooks

Alan McGowan
In Arcadia

M Oils

B Jacket illustration
to reflect the elusive
and magical search
for Arcadia in
Ben Okri's novel

C Nick Castle
F Orion Books

Gunnlaug Moen Hembery
'Mmm'

M   Pen, ink, digital

B   Illustrations for a cook
book that is aimed
at people moving
away from home –
the illustration is for a
chapter called 'Food
for the Dating Game'

C   CesilieTanderø

F   Salsa Forlag

Richard Myers
Platform 5

M Mixed media

B To produce images
based on different
aspects of travelling
by train, for a limited
edition book

DO NOT CROSS LINE   DO NOT CROSS LINE

Laurie Rosenwald

S Snobbery

M Mixed media

B 'Snobbery' by
Joseph Epstein,
tackling issues of
snobbery in the USA

S

C Martha Kennedy

F Houghton Mifflin

Rachel Ross

My Family and
Other Animals

M Gouache

B Audio cassette
sleeve cover image
of Gerald Durrell's
enchanting book

A Christmas Carol

M Gouache

B Compact disc sleeve
cover image of
Charles Dickens'
classic book

C Matt Bookman

F BBC Radio Collection

BBC Audiobooks

C Matt Bookman

F BBC Cover to Cover

BBC Audiobooks

Susan Scott
Sherlock Holmes and
the Blue Diamond

M   Pencil

B   For cover of book,
provide striking image
of Sherlock Holmes
examining a stolen
blue diamond, while
Watson looks on

C   Donna Thynne
Suzanne Williams

F   Oxford University Press
ELT Readers

Susan Scott
The Borrowers' House

M Pencil

B Cutaway house
showing "Borrowers"
living in real people's
house (period 1950s)
to aid students'
understanding
of prepositions eg.
on, under, behind etc.

C Carole Edwards

F Oxford University Press
ELT

Anders Westerberg

Persuading
Editor McArdle

Challenger's Crossing

M Watercolour, ink

B Illustrations for
'The Lost World' by
Arthur Conan Doyle

C Donna Thynne
F Oxford University Press

Jonathan Williams
Miracle Escape
on Highway 54

M Digital

B Woodrow Creekmore,
standing by the side
of his wrecked vehicle,
accounts for a
miraculous escape
to Sergeant Fishbein

C Alison Wright

F Oxford University Press

Samantha Wilson
Parties

M Mixed media

B Illustration for a
double page spread
chapter opener, in
semi-silhouette style,
from 'Domestic Bliss'
by Rita Konig

C Denise Bates

F Ebury Press

Samantha Wilson
After Dinner Treats

M Mixed media

B Illustration for a
double page spread
chapter opener, in
semi-silhouette style,
from 'Domestic Bliss'
by Rita Konig

C Denise Bates

F Ebury Press

Student
Gold award winner

Keiko Asahina

G   Mind

M   Mixed media

B   To produce a
series of images for
Arthur Bradford's
book 'Dogwalker'

G

Kath Allsopp
Untitled 1,2

M Acrylic, collage

B A personal project
which was to create
a series of illustrations
examining aspects
of communication

Jane Armistead
Hands

M Watercolour

B Illustration
showing the use
of sign language
spelling 'sign'

Keiko Asahina

Moonlight		A Sign	Turn Left	Desire
Chess Game	**M**	Pencil drawing		
M Acrylic	**B**	To focus on		
B To create surreal		relationships		
world with animals		between people		
		and the city,		
		and explore the		
		narrative aspects		
		within the theme		

Emma Bray
Fish Restaurant   Home   Loyola Law School   Space Centre
M Mixed media
B A collection of
stamps illustrating
the architecture
of Frank Gehry

Scott Byrne-Fraser
All Terrain
Scout Transport

M Digital

B To produce a short
computer based
animation featuring
a 3D model of the
AT-ST 'Chicken
Walker' to promote
the launch of DVD
computer game

Chris Cowdrill
Productive Day

M Mixed media, digital
B Self promotional
   experimental work

Ian Dodds

41 Winks

M   Digital

B   To illustrate an
article about lying
in – conditions have
to be met – warm
air, warm body,
warm bed = fug.
If any are missing
then it's just a nap

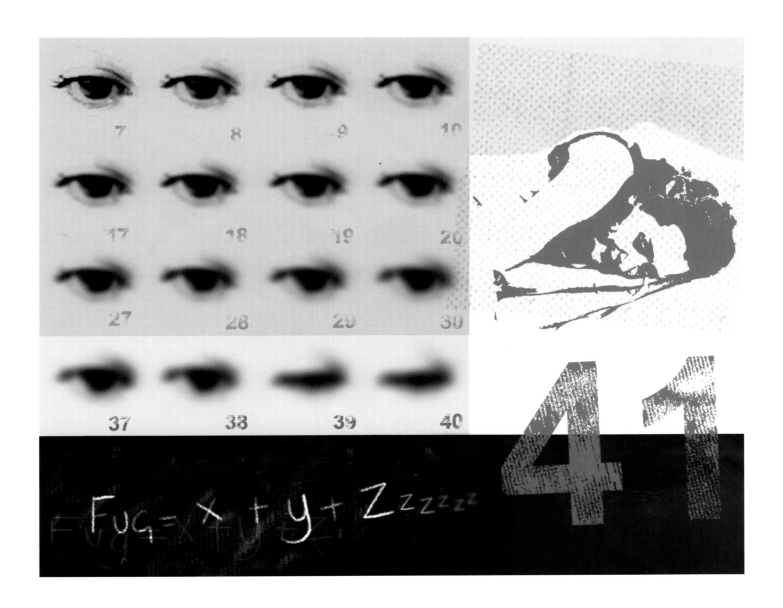

John Fox
Supermarine
Spitfire Mk XIX

M Digital

B To produce highly
detailed images
including computer
based 3D model
for inclusion in a
poster celebrating
the historical
Spitfire aeroplane

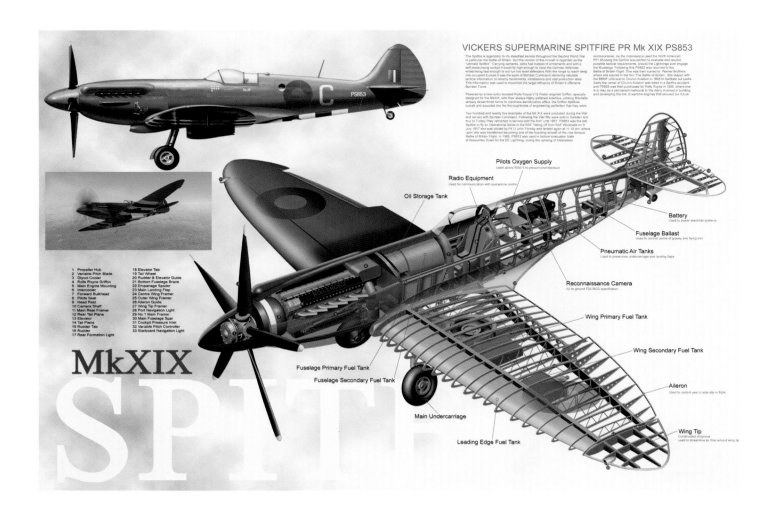

Philip Grayston
Cobra

M   Digital

B   To profile computer
generated 3D
model of AC Cobra
for inclusion in an
interactive CD-ROM
promoting the car

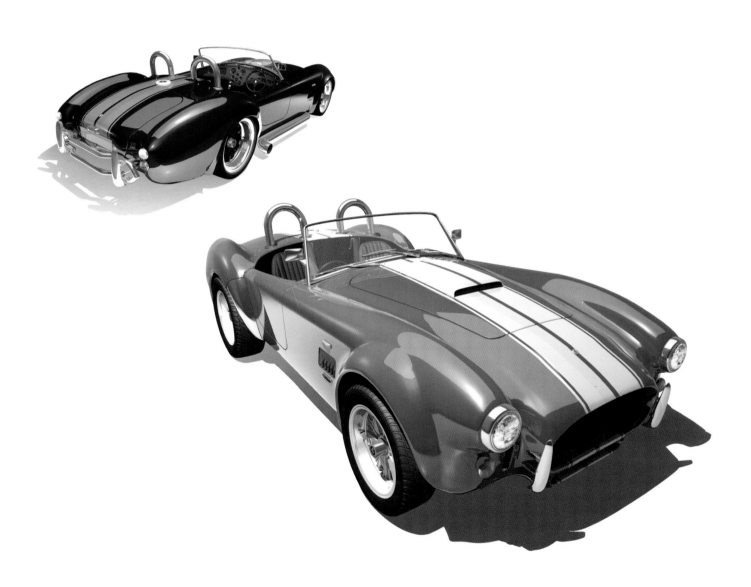

Elaine Hedges

Will it be Soon?

M Watercolour

B To produce a picture
book with therapeutic
value around the
world of an adopted
or fostered child
and the insecurities
that they may suffer
from as a result

Paul Jackson

On the Road		The Bad Sermon
M Photocopy, omnicrom	**M**	Photocopy, omnicrom
B Create a series of illustrations that represent the beginning, middle and end of the novel 'On the Road', by Jack Kerouac	**B**	Notion of the Western – exploring the visual cliché of spaghetti westerns, and inherent narrative and visual signatures

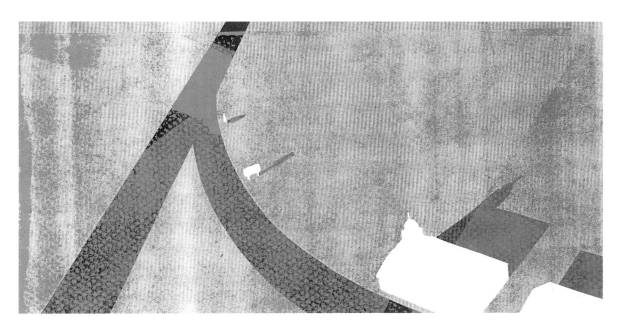

Katherina Manolessou

S Date Me!

M Screenprint

B Double spread
from stickerbook
'It's Love' based on
Lovehearts sweets.
Here, the couple
obsess about each
other and prepare
for their first date

Untitled

M Screenprint

B The inhabitants
of a big city decide
to 'get out more'

S

S

Kate Milner
The Patriarch

M Ink drawing,
photogram

B Part of a student
project about
celebrity, faith and
tribalism based on
the biblical stories
in Genesis

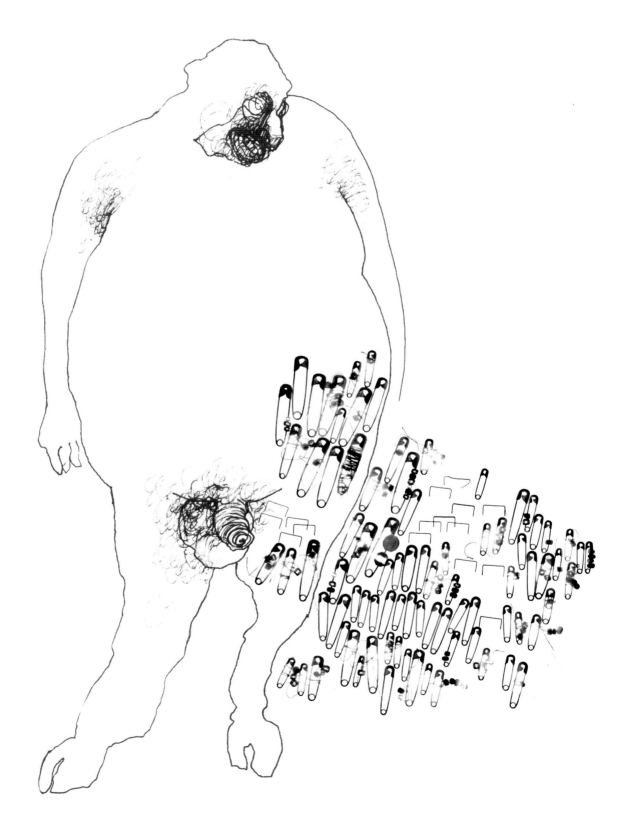

Kate Milner
Daddy Bear, Mummy
Bear, Baby Bear

M Collaged ink drawing,
photogram

B Part of a student
project on suburban
housing estates

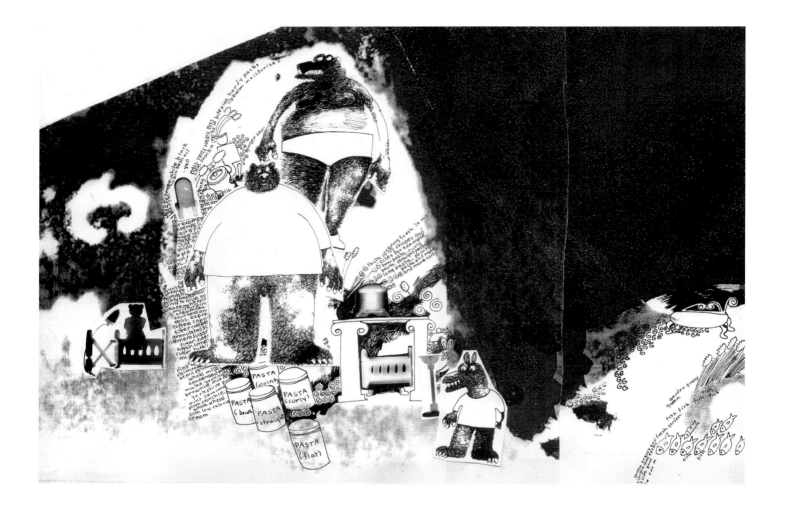

Jenny Rushton

B   Men in Skirts 1,2

M   Mixed media

B   Provide imagery
to accompany the
V&A 'Men in Skirts'
exhibition. Self
initiated masculine/
feminine project

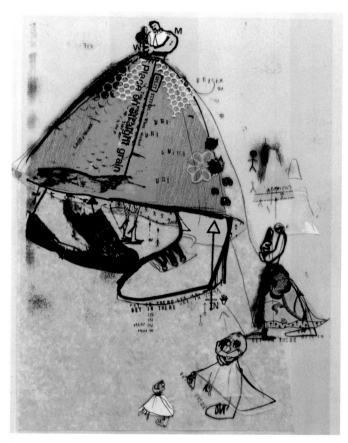
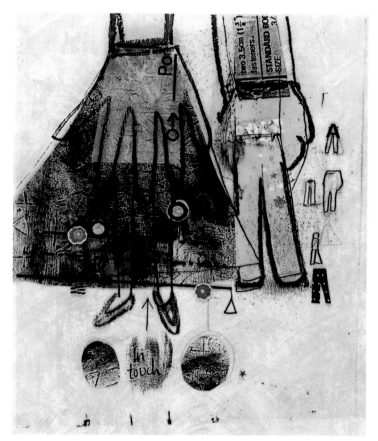

B

Philip Smith
Girl with Reflection

M   Multimedia

B   Part of a full length
study, the piece
contains a narrative
of its own, left
open for the view
to contemplate
themselves

Julia Staite

Pig on the Bone   I wasn't Scared

M   Mixed media

B   One of twelve double
page illustrations for a
story written by myself
as a child called 'The
Day the Dinosaur
came to Kilham'

Sharon Tancredi

Escapism

M Collage, mixed media

B An image that
illustrates the
idea of escapism

Christine Thurston
No. 758,000,001
Perfect

M   Acrylic

B   An illustration in
response to the
use of biotechnology
in farm animals

Chris Watson
Big Red

M Mixed media

B Dust jacket for children's picture book, work in progress. A 21st century Red Riding Hood strays off the pavement

Naomi Tipping
Peas in a Pod

M Mixed media

B One illustration from a set of greeting cards with unusual messages. Text inside reads 'Congratulations on being the same'

Jessica Webster
Flying in Cakey Island

M   Acrylic

B   A page from my book
'Cakey Island', where
a little girl, Alice is
told by her Grandma
about an island where
cakes are made

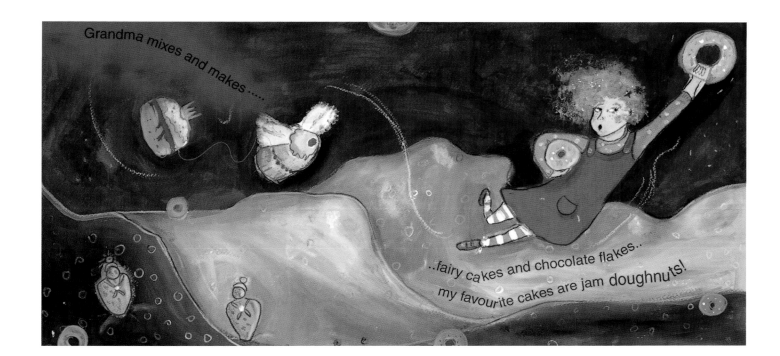

Philip Wrigglesworth

Animal Farm:
Illustration 6

M Acrylic, collage
B The farm puppies
have been taken
to the loft, to be
trained to hate and
attack Snowball

Love Predator:
No.5

M Acrylic, collage
B The female love
predator is lining
up her next victim

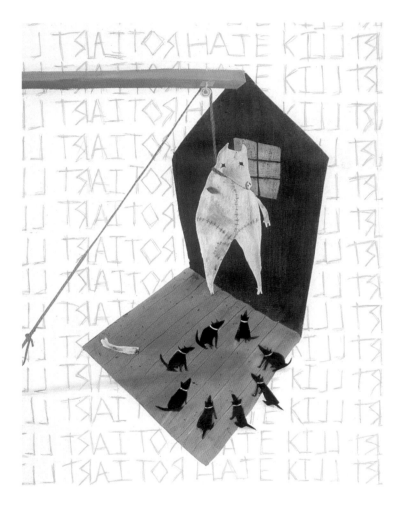

Unpublished
Gold award winner

Russell Cobb
G New Brain
Shaped Teabags
M Acrylic
B Number 16 in a
series of unique
and collectable
postcards sent to
clients. Depicts the
illustrator's unusual
brewing thoughts
and refreshing
illustration taste

G

A. Richard Allen
Elephant Man

M Ink, digital

B Self promotional,
postcard image

186

Katherine Baxter
Simply Culture

M Mixed media

B To produce an artwork,
suitable for use as a
poster for Transport
for London, designed
to inform all Londoners
of their rich cultural
heritage and the
current cultural
output of London.

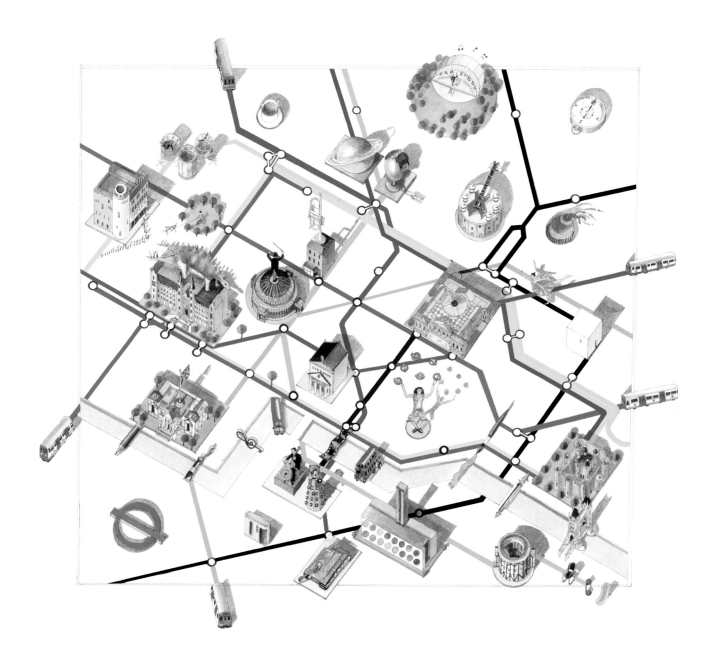

Justine Beckett
The Green Shoe
M Original art, digital
B Personal thought

David Bimson

Give Thanks
to the Yanks

M Gouache

B To illustrate how
traditional European
eating habits are
being infiltrated by
an American lifestyle

Bedroom Boredom

M Gouache

B Speculative image
to illustrate an article
concerning marital
relationships

Paul Bommer
A Midsummer
Night's Dream

M Digital

B Self promotional
piece to illustrate a
poster/book cover for
the Shakespeare play,
focusing on the key
character of Puck

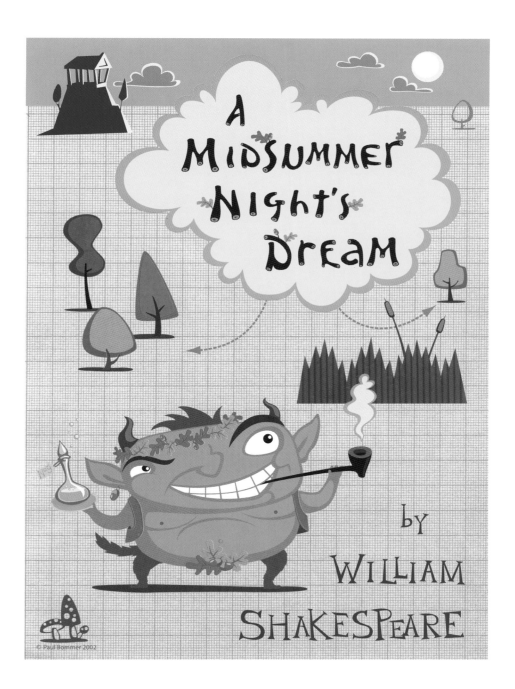

John Bradley
Freddie

M Ink, digital
B Self promotional

Michael Bramman
Cheyenne

M Acrylic

B Promotional

Anthony Branch

Solomon Grundy (Sunday)

Who Killed Cock Robin?

M Digital

B Personal brief – noir nursery rhymes

David Bray
12 People you Might
Like to Meet
M Original art, digital
B To show the cultural
diversity of London

Derek Brazell
Bandana Anya

M Gouache, pencil

B To illustrate a
contemporary kid in
a cool, attractive way

David Broadbent

B Blue Teeth

M Acrylic

B Creation of an
image to illustrate
the success of
Blue Tooth technology

B

Hazel Natasha Brook
Dampened
M Mixed media
B One of 15 illustrations
   for a forthcoming
   book project of 20th
   century poems on
   the themes of liberty
   and the environment.
   Dampened is inspired
   by a Paul Eluard poem

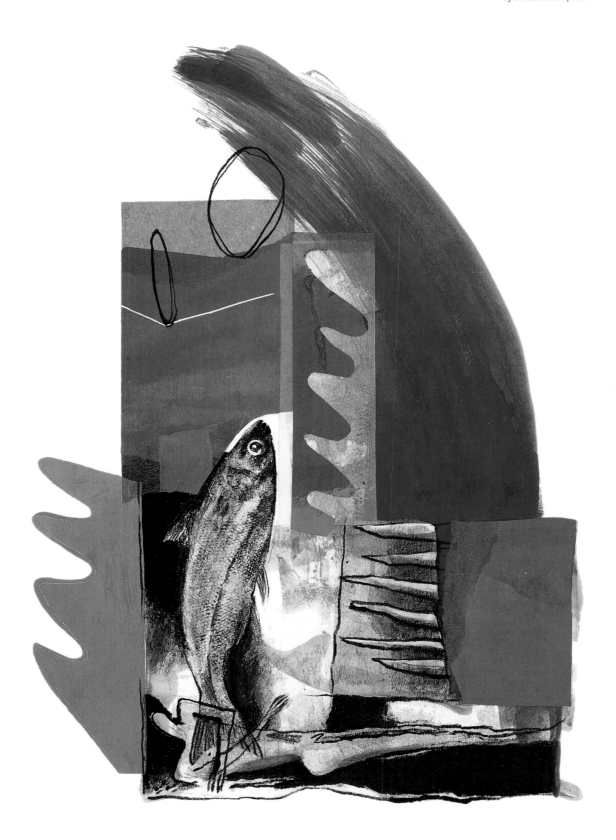

Hazel Natasha Brook

Perspective

M   Mixed media

B   Perspective is
inspired by a
Federico Lorca poem

Paul Brown

Nightmare

M   Mixed media

B   Image of person
troubled by nightmares

Matthew Buckingham
5 Chickens and
Cunning Mr Fox 1,2,3

M Watercolour, ink

B To illustrate text
from my own
children's book

Finn Campbell Notman
S Writer's Block
M Digital
B Editorial piece
for an article
on writer's block

Graham Carter
S Space Bears
M Original art, digital
B Personal thought

S

Marina Caruso
Mercury Fillings
M Digital
B The dangers of
   the toxic fillings in
   our mouths and
   natural ways of
   chelating mercury
   from the body

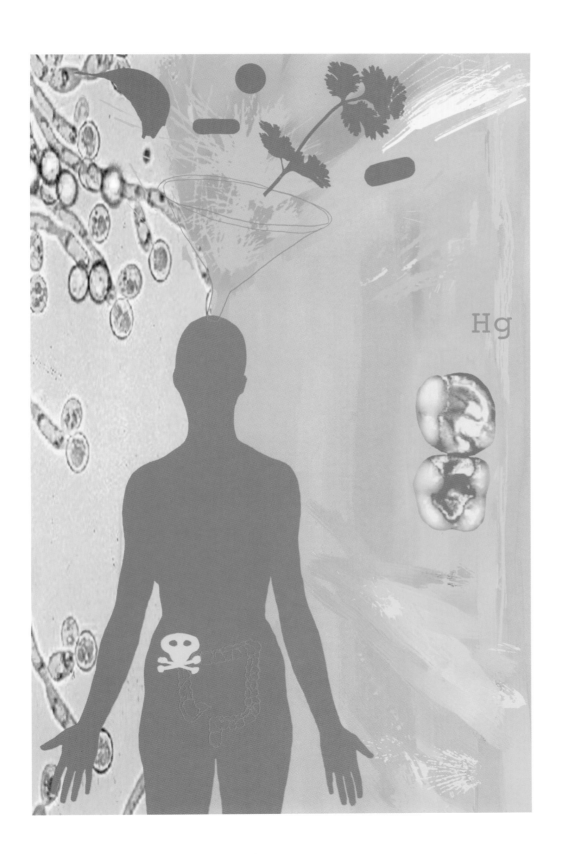

Scott Chambers

Sound Check   Shopping for Love   Car Wash

M Mixed media

B Self promotional work

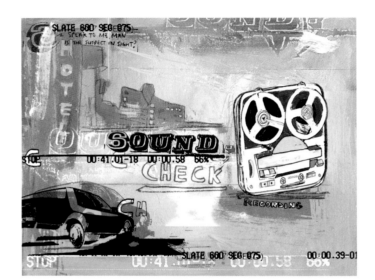

John Charlesworth
Perestroika-Lypse Now

M   Digital

B   One of a series
of short personal
promotional pieces,
fusing together the
two elements of
socialist art and
commercial Disney
influence

204

Chiara
Tea Time
Monster Manners

M Mixed media

B A monster with
impeccable manners
and his dealings
with a mischievous
miss – afternoon tea
is disastrous

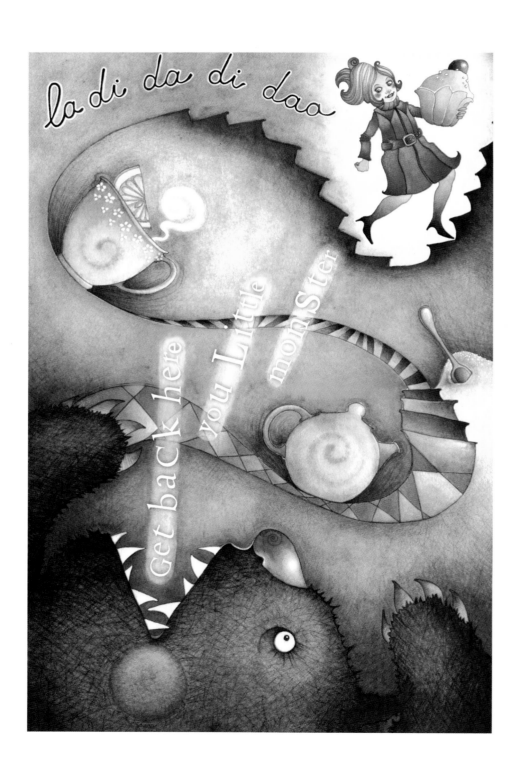

Russell Cobb

New Robo Flakes

M Acrylic

B Number 19 in a
series of unique and
collectable postcards
sent to clients.
Based on the theme
of breakfast cereals
encouraging clients
to consume

Cobbacetomol

M Acrylic

B Number 20 depicts
the illustrator as
the perfect cure for
difficult commissions

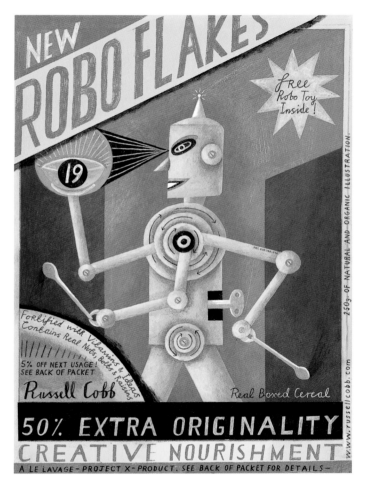

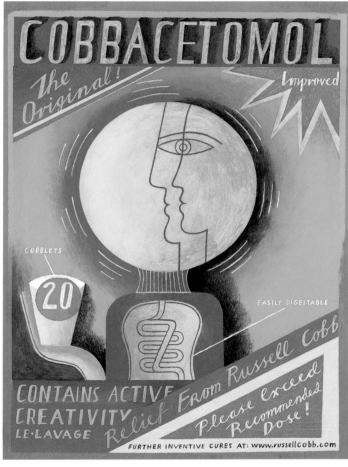

Russell Cobb

Revealing Shop
Fronts

M Acrylic

B Number 22 in a
series of unique and
collectable postcards
sent to clients. Based
on the theme of shop
fronts encouraging
commissioners
to shop at
www.russellcobb.com

The Cobblex Watchface

M Acrylic

B Number 17 depicts
the illustrator as
a multi-functioned
and durable deep
sea divers watch

Action Cobb

M Acrylic

B Number 23 depicts
the illustrator as a multi
function action toy

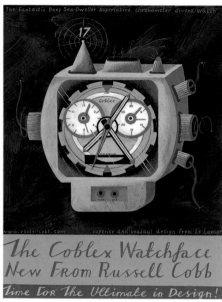

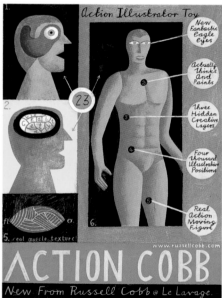

Lucy Couchman
Never Cook Aunts
in a Frying Pan

M   Collage, pencil

B   To produce a full page
illustration for the
poem 'Uncle James'
by Margaret Mahy

Jonathan Croft
The Wasp Factory
M Mixed media
B Book cover for the
novel by Iain Banks

Jonathan Cusick
Porterhouse Blue

M Acrylic

B Book cover for the
novel by Tom Sharpe

C Bob Hollingsworth

F Random House

Barry Downard
Chicken Home
M Mixed media
B Self initiated
book project

Camilla Jane Dowse
The Brush Shop
M   Ink, pencil
B   Self promotional work

Susan Duxbury-Hibbert
Pease Porridge Hot
M   Collage
B   Part of a self
promotional series
illustrating nursery
rhymes, featuring
a recurring family
of characters

Pease porridge hot,
Pease porridge cold,
Pease porridge in the pot,
Nine days old . . .

Alison Edgson
Spear Thistle

M Watercolour
B Personal promotion

Nicola Edwards
Simply Culture

M Acrylic

B To produce an artwork,
suitable for use as a
poster for Transport
for London, designed
to inform all Londoners
of their rich cultural
heritage and the
current cultural
output of London.

Max Ellis
Enduring

M Digital

B Exhibition piece
portraying the
enduring figure
of womanhood.
The eyes in the
locks looking out
unable to perceive
the beauty of the
enduring figure

Lynn Evans
Almond Coffee

M Lino cut, gouache

B One of a series
of illustrations
depicting a range
of flavoured coffees

Cathy Gale
Simply Culture

M Gouache, collage

B To produce an artwork,
suitable for use as a
poster for Transport
for London, designed
to inform all Londoners
of their rich cultural
heritage and the
current cultural
output of London.

Paul Garland
It's got a Bit
of a Kick to it!
M   Digital, mixed media
B   Promotional piece

C   Heike Rochau
F   Sieger Design
for Ritzenhoff

Phil Garner

Empire

M Pen, ink, watercolour

B To produce poster
size images of some
of my favourite icons

Four, Four, Two

M Acrylic on board

B One of a series of
paintings evoking
childhood memories.
In this instance, the
'wannabe' England
coach/games teacher
on the school field

Christopher Gibbs
The Cat Burglar

M   Digital

B   A play on words about
a dog who steals
cats, for a possible
children's book

Rachel Goslin
Woody Allen

M   Mixed media

B   A portrait/caricature
of Woody Allen for
use in editorial press

Willi Gray
Peter and the Wolf

M   Drawing, digital

B   Self promotional
piece – was the
boy who cried wolf
a lycanthrope?

Nicola Gregory
Pears
M Watercolour
B Personal work

Peter Grundy
Commuter

M Digital

B To produce an artwork,
suitable for use as a
poster for Transport
for London, designed
to inform all Londoners
of their rich cultural
heritage and the
current cultural
output of London.

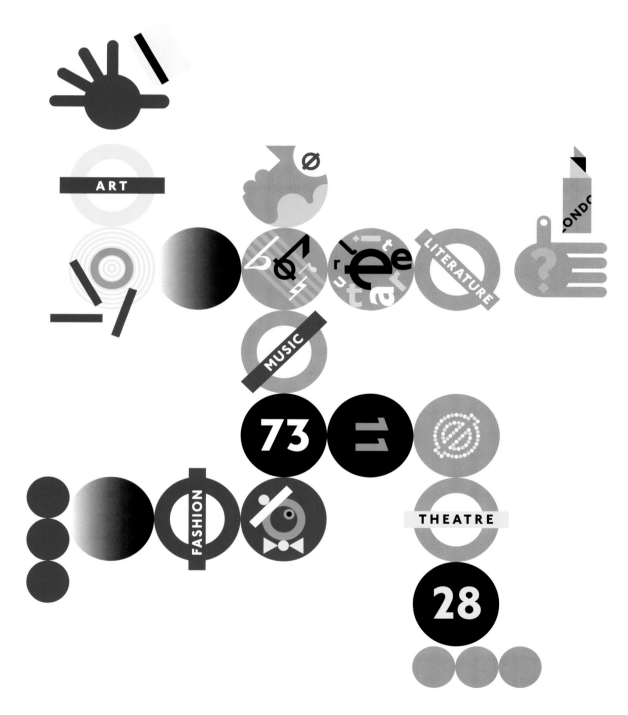

F Society of
Artists Agents

Bernard Gudynas
Simply Culture

M Digital

B To produce an artwork,
suitable for use as a
poster for Transport
for London, designed
to inform all Londoners
of their rich cultural
heritage and the
current cultural
output of London.

Itchy Animation
Hip Hop Hardman
M Digital
B A commission for
Select magazine
article on hip hop
stereotypes and
personalities

Kevin Hauff
Sat-Car
M Mixed media
B Image exploring the
benefits of satellite
navigation for the
average commuter
in getting from A to B

Tony Healey
Hooker

M Ink, watercolour

B Personal promotional
illustration of
Blues legend,
John Lee Hooker

Naomi Hocking
Buildings of
my Travels

M   Painter

B   Research and
experimentation for
travel illustration

Alan Heighton
The Geometry
of Chance

M   Digital

B   Self promotional
work to illustrate
the madness of
activity that could
happen in the city

David Holmes
Blue Plant

M Watercolour, crayon

B One of a series of 15
postcards to promote
a private exhibition

Helen J Holroyd
Knock, Knock!
M   Ink, digital
B   Self promotional

Darren Hopes
Child 1
M   Mixed media
B   Self promotional

Jane Human
The Morning After

M   Oil, graphite

B   Experimental work
used as a promotional
Christmas card.
Ongoing personal
project on coastlines

Rod Hunt

Robotics

M Digital

B Self promotional

Great Apes

M Digital

B A cover for 'Great
Apes' by Will Self

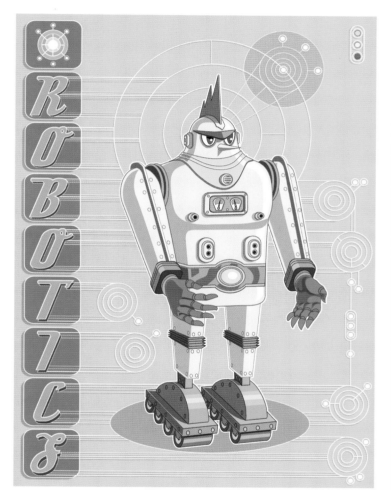

Ashley Hutchinson
Sausages!

M Lino print

B Self promotional

Richard Johnson

Ash Tray Gob

M   Acrylic

B   Self promotional
    illustration – to
    produce conceptual
    images illustrating
    negative aspects
    of smoking

Leave the Light On

M   Acrylic

B   Self promotional
    image – to produce
    a dark illustration
    that still remains
    child-friendly

Jean-Christian Knaff
Image for TFL
Competition
M Acrylic, mixed media
B To produce an artwork,
suitable for use as a
poster for Transport
for London, designed
to inform all Londoners
of their rich cultural
heritage and the
current cultural
output of London

Sarah Lawrence
Mermaid
M Watercolour
B Personal work

Matt Lee
Stress

M   Mixed media

B   From a series of 100
character drawings
on a mental health
theme – used for an
informative booklet
about stress

Ollie Lett
Love Cats

M   Acrylic

B   To produce a piece
of work suitable for
card / stationery /
calendar use

Henning Löhlein
Merry Xmas

M Acrylic

B Self promotional
Christmas card

Frank Love

War with the Newts

M Mixed media

B Front cover for
Capek's novel where
intelligent reptiles
are discovered and
exploited

Patent Pending No.12

M Mixed media

B A series of inventions
for modern living
e.g. 'Easi-Bolt'
portable scenery

236

Patrick MacAllister
Simply Culture

M Ink, digital

B To produce an artwork,
   suitable for use as a
   poster for Transport
   for London, designed
   to inform all Londoners
   of their rich cultural
   heritage and the
   current cultural
   output of London.

Ric Machin
Marlon Brando

M Oils

B Self promotional

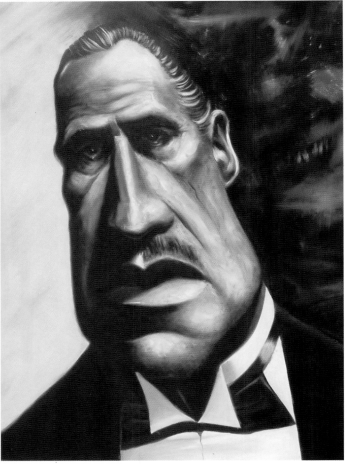

Ian Mack

The Road to Dolly	Phobias
M Digital	M Digital
B Editorial piece to illustrate an article about the manipulation of genes	B Portfolio piece to illustrate phobias

THE ROAD TO DOLLY

Dan McFadden

Journey

M   Acrylic, collage

B   An editorial piece
    on homelessness
    and how the burden
    can be felt not only
    by the person in
    question but also
    his loved ones

Shane Mc Gowan

Evie Dancing

M   Digital

B   Page from an
    as yet unfinished
    children's book
    about a little girl who
    has a big adventure
    'down under'

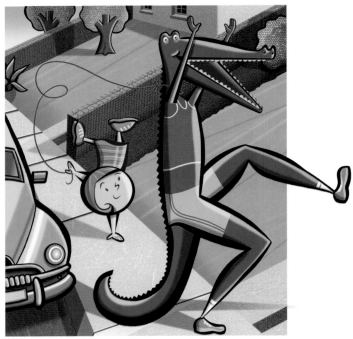

Simply Culture

M   Digital

B   To produce an artwork,
suitable for use as a
poster for Transport
for London, designed
to inform all Londoners
of their rich cultural
heritage and the
current cultural
output of London.

Kate Miller
Together
M Digital
B To produce a series
of images for an
advertising pitch,
to describe the spirit
of the company
'Diageo' focusing
on the employees

C Rob Lamb
F Addison Corporate
Marketing

David Martin Morrison
Euro Titanic?

M Digital

B Personal promotional
work – how the Euro
may fail when up
against the US dollar

242

Kevin O'Brien
Home Visit

M Pen, digital

B To illustrate
a story about a
retired scientist

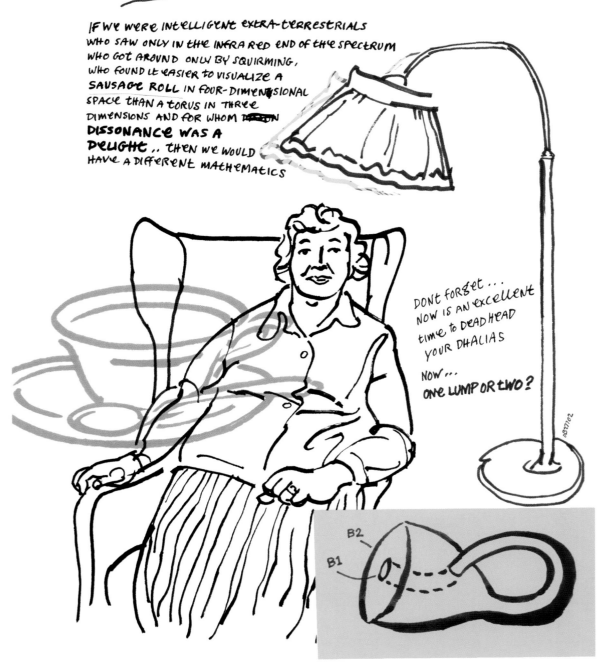

Kevin O'Keefe
Christmas Episode

M Pen, digital

B I was fed up with
smarmy Christmas
cards, I hate snow and
I don't trust turkeys,
so I drew my own
seasons greetings

Paquebot
Park

M Digital

B Scene of a park with
strange characters as
promotional showcase

Mr. Right
M Digital
B A woman thinks
she found
Mr. Right for her

Jacqui Paull
Cuba

M Original art,
   photo, digital

B Personal thoughts
   about Cuba

Sally Pinhey
Arum Italicum

M Watercolour

B To illustrate
Arum Italicum from
the Chelsea Physic
Garden for storage
in archives with dried
specimen for DNA

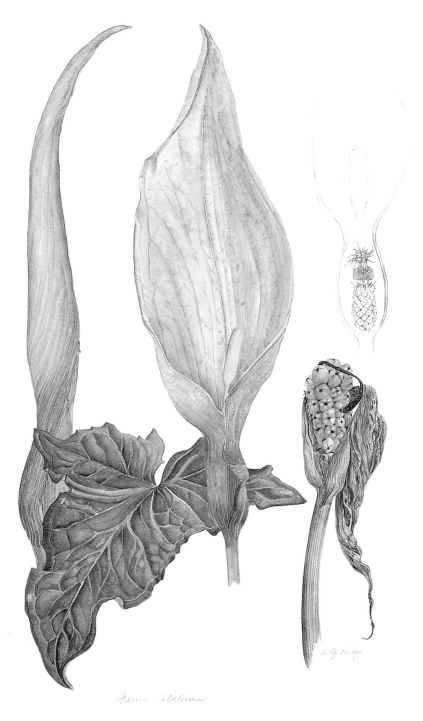

Arum italicum

C Rosie Atkins

F Chelsea Physic
Garden

Christopher Rainham
Angel

M   Acrylic, conté, gold leaf
B   Experimental design
    for greetings card

Catell Ronca
Untitled
M Mixed media
B Self promotional work

Michael Sheehy
Doctor Love
M Mixed media
B A heartthrob
doctor in a TV
medical drama
looks unusually
like Dr Spock

C Tracey Gardiner
F Radio Times

RadioTimes

Lorna Siviter
Boy Racer

M   Digitally manipulated
     collage

B   Personal promotional
     work – part of a series
     inspired by things that
     I find amusing

Anna Steinberg
Katrine's Coat

M Ink

B Personal project
based on overheard
conversations

Deborah Stephens
Simply Culture

M Oils

B To produce an artwork,
suitable for use as a
poster for Transport
for London, designed
to inform all Londoners
of their rich cultural
heritage and the
current cultural
output of London.

Andrew Steward
Red Ken

M Mixed media

B Illustrate
Ken Livingston's
frustration over
the issue of PPP
for London Transport

Michelle Thompson
Dog

M Collage

B Self promotion

Mark Thurgood

Head and Shoulders

M Aluminium / pewter /
steel / brass / gold leaf

B Details from a 3D
construction to be
used throughout
a major advertising
campaign, elevating
the product to be
'above the rest'

The Gardener's Way

M Mixed media

B To produce a title
header for continuous
use on a monthly
magazine

Erica Wakerly
Home: Fun

M Fabric, collage

B To illustrate the
modern home as
a place to have fun

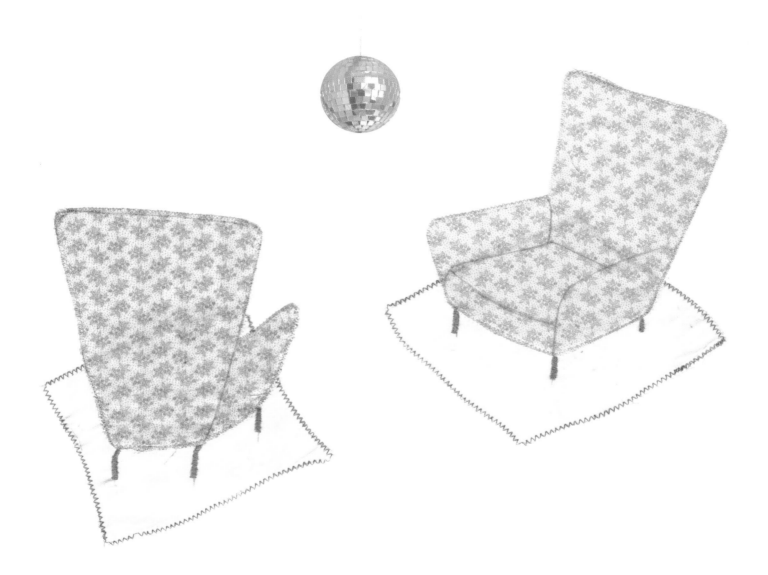

Stephen Waterhouse
Simply Culture

M Digital

B To produce an artwork,
suitable for use as a
poster for Transport
for London, designed
to inform all Londoners
of their rich cultural
heritage and the
current cultural
output of London.

Chris Watson
Vote Bob

M Silkscreen print

B Election poster
for Bob Dobbs'
Free Party

Alex Whitworth
Moses

M Mixed media

B Personal project to
illustrate the Orwell
classic, Animal Farm

C Bob Dobbs

F Free Party

Jonathan Williams
Gordo's Budget
Hits Men for Six

M Digital

B 2002, an excellent
budget for trannies:
the cost of fags, beers,
petrol and betting
went up, while taxes
on lipstick, tampons
and tights went down

Dare to be a Daniel

M Digital

B As New Labour
spins out of control,
Tony Benn emerges
as a voice in the
wilderness

Sharon Williams
Rainy Day McKinley

M Acrylic

B Fun and games
on a rainy day.
Speculative piece
for a children's book

Alan Young
Café de la
Chanterelle 1

Concours Fédéral
d'Hiver

M   Digital

B   For projected book:
digitally developed
drawings (made at
events where cameras
are not tolerated)
to accompany text
documenting
eyewitness experience
of cock fighting
in France

C   Randal Cooke
Philip Bennetta

F   PROOF @ KIAD
for The Community of
Poets & Artists Press

AOI **membership** benefits

The Association of Illustrators provides a voice for professional illustrators and by force of numbers and expertise is able to enforce the rights of freelance illustrators at every stage of their careers. Membership of the AOI is open to all illustrators, illustration students, agents, lecturers and illustration clients.

All categories of membership receive the following benefits:
- Bi-monthly journal
- Discounted rate for Images – call for entries, hanging fees and annual pages
- Contact details on office database for enquiries from clients
- Discounts from material suppliers
- Regional group contacts
- Discounts on AOI events and publications

In addition we provide the following services for particular types of membership:

Full membership
This category is for professional illustrators who have had work commissioned and accept the AOI code of conduct:

- Legal advice on contracts
- Hotline information on pricing and professional practice
- Free portfolio surgery
- Business advice – an hour's free consultation with a chartered accountant on accounts, book-keeping, National Insurance, VAT and tax
- Full members are entitled to use the affix 'Mem AOI'
- Discounts on AOI events and publications

Associate membership
This one-year category is for newcomers and illustrators on their first year out of college who have not published work. In exceptional circumstances this membership can be extended by an extra year:
- Hotline information on pricing and professional practice
- Free portfolio surgery
- Business advice – an hour's free consultation with a chartered accountant on accounts, book-keeping, National Insurance, VAT and tax
- Legal advice on contracts

Student membership
This service is for students on full-time illustration or related courses:
- See above services for all AOI members
- Free portfolio surgery

Corporate membership
This service is for agents and clients from the illustration industry:
- Bi-monthly journal
- Free copy of the Images catalogue
- All corporate members' staff and illustrators will receive discounts on events, Images and AOI publications

For an application form and cost details please contact:
Association of Illustrators
81 Leonard Street
London EC2A 4QS

T +44 (0)20 7613 4328
F +44 (0)20 7613 4417

E info@a-o-illustrators.demon.co.uk
W www.theAOI.com

College membership
College membership entitles the college to the following benefits:
- Bi-monthly journal
- Large discounts on AOI events and publications
- Link to college web page from AOI site
- Copy of Images illustration annual
- The right to use the AOI member logo on publicity

Additional options (at extra cost) include:
- Portfolio consultations
- Illustrator lecture
- Discount on bulk orders of additional copies of the bi-monthly journal, Rights & Survive
- Degree show presence on AOI website

AOI publications
Survive: The Illustrators Guide to a Professional Career
Published by the AOI and revised 2001, Survive is the only comprehensive and in-depth guide to illustration as a professional career. Established illustrators, agents, clients and a range of other professionals have contributed to this fourth edition. Each area of the profession including portfolio presentation, self promotion and copyright issues are looked at in detail. The wealth of information in Survive makes it absolutely indispensable to the newcomer and also has much to offer the more experienced illustrator.

Rights: The Illustrators Guide to Professional Practice
Rights is an all inclusive guide to aspects of the law specifically related to illustration. It includes information about copyright, contracts, book publishing agreements, agency agreements, how to go about seeking legal advice, how to calculate fees and guidance on how to write a licence. Rights is the result of a number of years research. It has been approved by solicitors and contains the most detailed and accurate model terms and conditions available for use by illustrators or clients.

Troubleshooting Guide
A handbook written by solicitors Ruth Gladwin and Robert Lands (Finers Stephens Innocent) covering essential legal issues surrounding subjects such as animation, collage, websites, and advice about taking cases to the small claims court.

Client Directories
Both Publishing and Editorial Directories list over 150 illustration clients with full contact details: the Advertising Directory holds details of over 150 advertising agencies who commission illustration – providing an invaluable source of information for all practitioners.

www.theaoi.com

www.theaoi.com was developed and launched in 2002. The intention being to create an all-encompassing resource which would be the first port of call for anyone interested in the business of illustration, from the client looking for a suitable illustrator to commission to the graduate looking to broaden their knowledge base. Evolving month on month the site currently features over 2500 pages divided into the following six sections.

Image File

Just launched, the AOI Image File is a database of published illustration work from all areas of the industry. Images are categorised according to their initial usage and tagged with the illustrator's e-mail address and URL. Features include:

- Favourites: Build an editable collection of favourite images (accessible anytime you return to the site) by simply checking the favourites box under the chosen illustration.
- E-mail: Favourites can be e-mailed to colleagues
- Rate It: Award a rating (out of 10) to a chosen image. Top rated images can be separately viewed.
- Top Hits: Illustration thumbnails which have been most clicked on can be viewed separately. Illustrators can add work at any time, full submission details are available on the site.

News and information

Regularly updated news page and full information about the Association. Sections include: Join, Personnel, Rights, Publications, Downloads etc.

Directory

An index of links to illustration related material on the web. The predominant section, illustrators, is intended as a client resource with each individual illustrator represented by a thumbnail and a direct link to their portfolio, whether on their own site or within their agent's or other corporate site. For a small fee illustrators have the option of enhancing their listing with a larger image and descriptive text. The Directory also contains comprehensive links to agents both in the UK and internationally. Links to advertising agencies, book publishers and other resources of interest to illustrators also feature.

Discussion

The Discussion Board is open to everyone to read and post. In order to post users are first required to register – a simple 2 minute process which asks that you adhere to our code of conduct. Once registered users can reply to existing messages or start new topics. Images and links also can be included with messages. The Board has eight forums, Professional Practice, AOI Feedback, Tools of the Trade, General, Archive, Polls (where users can vote on issues of the day) and a separate forum for AOI members only. The latest addition is Interview where live discussion can take place with specially invited industry figures. Brian Grimwood was our first guest in November 2002 and more are planned for the near future.

Images annual

Browse the last four annuals (included in their entirety) and check out the last 25 years in Images History complete with lists of participating illustrators and judges.

Articles

Archive of texts drawn predominantly from the AOI's Journal publication. Individual issues of the Journal can be browsed or search through the articles categorised under various industry headings i.e. agents, professional practice, legal, education etc.

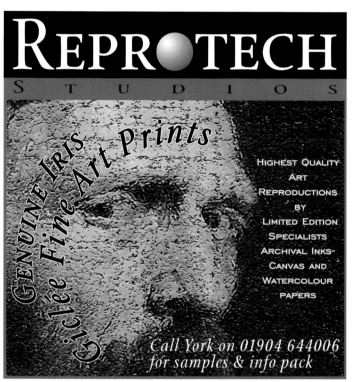
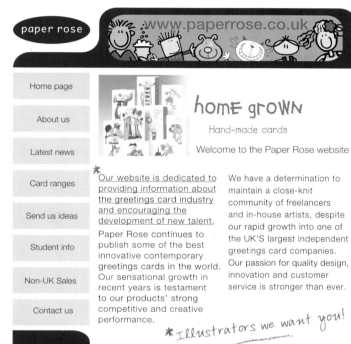

The AOI Journal

The essential illustration magazine

The AOI Journal, re-launched in Summer 2000, covers a wide range of issues related to the illustration industry including:

- Current industry affairs
- Illustration events
- Reviews
- Interviews
- Letters

Regular contributors include practitioners, educators and industry professionals. The Journal provides a forum for on-going debate, and a valuable insight into contemporary illustration.

Published six times a year. Free to members.
To subscribe to the AOI Journal as a non-member, please send your cheque for £30, made payable to the Association of Illustrators, to:

Journal Subscription
AOI
81 Leonard Street
London EC2A 4QS

For payment by Visa, Mastercard or Switch
T 020 7613 4328

The Society of Artist's Agents
Illustration Awards 2003/4

www.saaillustrationawards.com

London's Transport
Museum
Covent Garden Piazza

SOCIETY
OF
ARTISTS
AGENTS

www.theSAA.com

index of illustrators

Henning Löhlein 94,234
Centre Space
6 Leonard Lane
Bristol BS1 1EA
T 0117 929 9077
F 0117 929 9077
M 07711 285 202
E lohlein@aol.com
W www.lohlein.com

Leonie Lord 95
A The Inkshed
98 Columbia Road
London E2 7QB
T 020 7613 2323
W www.inkshed.co.uk

Frank Love 235
the dairy
5-7 Marischal Road
London SE13 5LE
T 020 8297 2212
F 020 8297 1680
M 07930 492 471
E thedairy@btclick.com
W www.franklove.co.uk
A Eastwing
98 Columbia Road
London E2 7QB
T 020 7613 5580
F 020 7613 2726
W www.eastwing.co.uk

Nick Lowndes 95
A Eastwing
98 Columbia Road
London E2 7QB
T 020 7613 5580
F 020 7613 2726
E andrea@eastwing.co.uk
W www.eastwing.co.uk

David Lyttleton 96
T 01704 530 407
E david.lyttleton@virgin.net

Patrick MacAllister 236
23 Vicars Oak Road
London SE19 1HE
T 020 8761 5578
F 020 8761 5578
E patrick.hat@talk21.com

Ric Machin 236
A Début Art
30 Tottenham Street
London W1T 4RJ
T 020 7636 1064
F 020 7580 7017
E debutart@coningsby
gallery.demon.co.uk
W www.debutart.com

Ian Mack 237
145 Dymchurch Road
Hythe, Kent CT21 6JU
T 01303 263 118
E ianmack@
btconnect.com

**Katherina
Manolessou** 172
85 Daley House
Du Cane Road
London W12 0UE
T 020 8740 4120
M 07903 124 821
E katherina@
lemoneyed.com
W www.lemoneyed.com

James Marsh 96
8 Cannongate Road
Hythe, Kent CT21 5PX
T 01303 263 118
F 01303 263 118
M 07973 114 019
E james@
james-marsh.co.uk
W www.jamesmarsh.com

Mark Marshall 133
Clockwork Studios
38a Southwell Road
London SE5 9PG
T 020 7924 0921
F 020 7924 0921
M 07985 648 655
E graphic_mm
@hotmail.com
A Eunice McMullen
Children's Literary Agent Ltd.
Low Ibbotsholme
Off Bridge Lane, Troutbeck
Bridge, Windemere
Cumbria LA23 1HU
T 01539 448 551

Mick Marston 46
6 Holtwood Road
Sheffield S4 7BA
T 0114 281 8440
M 07799 487 795
E mikiluv@blue
yonder.co.uk
W www.mikiluv.com
A Central Illustration Agency
36 Wellington Street
London WC2E 7BD
T 020 7240 8925
E info@central
illustration.com
W www.central
illustration.com

Jan Martin 97
32 Albert Park Place
Montpelier, Bristol BS6 5ND
T 0117 908 1675
M 07905 273 933
E j.martin1@blue
yonder.co.uk
W www.contact-
me.net/JanMartin

Richard May 98
T 020 7435 1681
020 7431 4525
E rich@richard-may.com
W www.richard-may.com

Steve May 98
A Arena
108 Leonard Street
London EC2A 4RH
T 020 7613 4040
F 020 7613 1441
E info@arenaworks.com
W www.arenaworks.com

Dan McFadden 238
24 Perseverance Street
Wyke, Bradford BD12 8BA
T 01274 607 180
M 07718 216 702
E dan@mcfaddens
place.fsnet.co.uk
W www.mcfaddens
place.fsnet.co.uk

John McFaul 99
8 Lumsden Terrace
Chatham, Kent ME4 6TN
T 01634 302 427
F 01634 302 495
M 07740 704 989
E pixelmcfaul@
blueyonder.co.uk
W www.pixelboy
mcfaul.co.uk
A Eastwing
98 Columbia Road
London E2 7QB
T 020 7613 5580
F 020 7613 2726
E andrea@eastwing.co.uk
W www.eastwing.co.uk

Alan McGowan 148
4F1, 3 Montgomery Street
Edinburgh EH7 5JU
T 0131 557 2396
M 07980 845 629
E mail@alanmcgowan.com
W www.illustrationart.net

Shane Mc Gowan
47, 238,239
23a Parkholme Road
London E8 3AG
T 020 7249 6444
F 020 7249 6444
M 07986 113 072
E shane.mcgowan
@virgin.net
A Three in a Box
468 Queen Street East
Suite 104, Box 03 Toronto
(ON) M5A 1T7 Canada
T 020 8853 1236

Sarah Mc Menemy 134
The Chocolate Factory
Clarendon Road
London N22 6XJ
T 020 8889 6682
M 07733 245 357
E sarah.mcmenemy
@virgin.net
A The Artworks
70 Rosaline Road
London SW6 7QT
T 020 7610 1801

Belle Mellor 100,101
Flat 3, 12 Lansdowne Street
Hove, East Sussex BN3 1FQ
T 01273 732 604
F 01273 732 604
M 07973 463 942
E belle.mellor@virgin.net
W www.bellemellor.com
A Three in a Box
468 Queen Street East
Suite 104, Box 03 Toronto
(ON) M5A 1T7 Canada
T 001 416 367 2446

Kate Miller 102,240
M 07958 998 078
E kate@hannayk.
freeserve.co.uk
A Central Illustration Agency
36 Wellington Street
London WC2E 7BD
T 020 7240 8925
E info@central
illustration.com
W www.central
illustration.com

Helen Mills 17
10 Radley Drive, Nuneaton
Warwickshire CV10 7HX
T 024 7634 6811
F 024 7637 1964
M 07811 882 126
E helen@helenmills.co.uk
W www.helenmills.co.uk
A Central Illustration Agency
36 Wellington Street
London WC2E 7BD
T 020 7240 8925
E info@central
illustration.com
W www.central
illustration.com

Kate Milner 173,174
3 Millbank, Leighton
Buzzard LU7 1AS
T 01525 382 545
E katemilner@yahoo.co.uk

**Gunnlaug Moen
Hembery** 103,149
M 07760 244 218
E post@gunnlaug.co.uk
W www.gunnlaug.co.uk
A Eye Candy
Illustration Agency
15 Frobisher Court
Sydenham Rise
London SE23 3XH
T 020 8291 0729
M 07811 363 718
E marc.lawrence@
eyecandy.co.uk
W www.eyecandy.co.uk

Lydia Monks 48,135
354 Manchester Road
Sheffield
South Yorkshire S10 5DQ
T 0114 268 2861
M 07971 052 529
E lydia@monks
24.demon.co.uk
A Hilary Delamere
The Agency, 24 Pottery Lane
London W11 4LZ
T 020 7727 1346

Jai Moodie 49
Studio 20/21
8 Lower Ormond Street
Manchester M1 5QF
T 0161 226 3715
F 0161 226 3715
M 07971 027 281
E jai.jams@good.co.uk
W www.jaimoodie.com

Tom Morgan-Jones 50
20 Tenison Road
Cambridge CB1 2DW
T 01223 305 424
M 07775 800 154
E tom@inkymess.com

**David Martin
Morrison** 241
20 Melrose Road, Pinner
Middlesex HA5 5RA
T 020 8868 4280
M 07980 028 235
E d4martin@hotmail.com
W www.dmmorrison.co.uk

Mary Murphy 136
c/o Tiffany Leeson
Egmont Books Ltd
239 Kensington High Street
London W8 6SA
T 020 7761 3500
F 020 7761 3510

Richard Myers 150
69 St. Catherine's Road
Harrogate HG2 8LA
T 01423 885 078
E richardmyers@talk21.com

Philip Nicholson 18
Torkel Jönsgård
S-430 10 Tvååker, Sweden
T 00 46 346 910 90
F 00 46 346 481 19
E philip@
illustrations.netg.se
W www.illustrations.se
A Thorogood Illustration
5 Dryden Street
London WC2E 9NW
T 020 8859 7507
020 8488 3195
W www.thorogood.net

Tilly Northedge 51
Grundy & Northedge
Power Road Studios
114 Power Road
London W4 5PY
T 020 8995 2452
E tilly@grundy
northedge.com
W www.grundy
northedge.com

Kevin O'Brien 242
Studio 355 Clerkenwell
Workshops
31 Clerkenwell Close
London EC1R 0AT
T 020 7278 2469
M 07815 579 293
E kevin.obrien7@virgin.net
W www.contact-
me.net/KevinO'Brien
A Black Hat
4 Northington Street
London WC1N 2JT
T 020 7430 9146
F 020 7430 9156
M 07711 034 890

Kevin O'Keefe 243
38 Osborne Road
Bristol BS3 1PW
T 0117 963 3835
F 0117 963 3835
M 07740 942 382
E jokevanoke@
blueyonder.co.uk

Mark Oldroyd 102
5 Harold Terrace, Battle
East Sussex TN33 0BP
T 01424 775 300
F 01424 775 300
M 07810 013 566

Dettmer Otto 103
300 North Street
Bristol BS3 1JU
M 07979 952 982
E otto@otto
illustration.com
W www.ottoillustration.com

Paquebot 103,244,245
Flat 2, 40 Tisbury Road
Hove, East Sussex BN3 3BA
T 01273 771 539
F 01273 771 539
E le.paquebot@virgin.net
W www.satillus.com

Steve Parkes 104
60 Belgravia House
London SW4 8HY
T 020 8674 2017
M 07885 035 624
E studio@stephen
parkes.com

Jackie Parsons 52
The Paperworks
Britannia Workshops
Waterworks Road, Hastings
East Sussex TN34 1RT
T 01424 441 972
F 01424 441 972
M 07957 121 818
E parsons@dircon.co.uk
A Central Illustration Agency
36 Wellington Street
London WC2E 7BD
T 020 7836 1106
E info@central
illustration.com
W www.central
illustration.com

Jacqui Paull 246
A Private View Art Agency
T 01743 350 355
E create@pvuk.com
W www.pvuk.com

Simon Pemberton 19,104
47 Turner Road
London E17 3JG
T 020 7923 9639
F 020 7923 9639
M 07976 625 802
E simon@simon
pemberton.com
W www.simon
pemberton.com

Beverly Philps 105
T 020 7978 8372
M 07811 909 279
E b.philp@virgin.net

Sally Pinhey 247
664 Dorchester Road
Upwey DT3 5LE
T 01305 813 307
F 01305 813 307
M 07719 923 434
E upwey.pinheys
@virgin.net
W www.sallypinhey.com

Ian Pollock 106
171 Bond Street
Macclesfield SK11 6RE
T 01625 426 205
F 01625 261 390
M 07770 927 940
E ianpllck@aol.com
A The Inkshed
98 Columbia Road
London E2 7QB
T 020 7613 2323
W www.inkshed.co.uk

Paul Powis 52
Four Seasons
Battenhall Avenue
Worcester WR5 2HW
T 01905 357 563
F 01905 357 563
E haywardpowis
@hotmail.com

Shonagh Rae 107
T 020 7739 7765
M 07768 742 275
E big.orange@virgin.net

Christopher Rainham 248
Acre House, Kiln Lane
Milnrow OL16 3TR
T 01706 868 577
F 01706 868 577
M 07786 686 776
E tlandale@
breathemail.net
W www.britart.com

Darren Raven 108
Happiness at Work
The Turks Head
1 Green Bank, Wapping
London E1W 2PA
T 020 7480 6364
F 020 7480 6364
M 07887 614 498
E darren@darrenraven.com
A Three in a Box
T 020 8853 1236
E www.threeinabox.com

**Maria
Raymondsdotter** 20
Stockholm Illustration
Stora Nygatan 44, S-111 27
Stockholm, Sweden
T 00 46 8 224 010
F 00 46 8 568 49960
M 00 46 70 491 8596
E maria@stockholm
illustration.com
W www.raymonds
dotter.com
A Central Illustration Agency
36 Wellington Street
London WC2E 7BD
T 020 7240 8925
E info@central
illustration.com
W www.central
illustration.com

Nathan Reed 137
Happiness at Work
The Turks Head
1 Green Bank, Wapping
London E1W 2PA
M 07899 088 406
E nathanreed25
@hotmail.com

Lucy Richards 137
A Frances McKay
Illustrations
14a Ravensdon Street
London SE11 4AR
T 020 7820 6203

Matthew Richardson 109
Garden Cottage, Penpont
Brecon, Powys LD3 8EU
T 01874 636 269
F 01874 636 269
E matthewxr@aol.com
A Eastwing
98 Columbia Road
London E2 7QB
T 020 7613 5580
F 020 7613 2726
W www.eastwing.co.uk

Catell Ronca 249
Happiness at Work
The Turks Head
1 Green Bank, Wapping
London E1W 2PA
M 07941 323 204
E catellronca@hotmail.com

David Rooney 110
Moss End, Rocky Valley
Kilmacanogue
County Wicklow, Ireland
T 00 353 1 274 0400
F 00 353 1 274 0400
M 00 353 8 7266 5524
E lofthouse@eircom.net

Laurie Rosenwald 151
A Début Art
30 Tottenham Street
London W1T 4RJ
T 020 7636 1064
F 020 7580 7017
E debutart@coningsby
gallery.demon.co.uk
W www.debutart.com

Rachel Ross 152
A The Inkshed
98 Columbia Road
London E2 7QB
T 020 7613 2323
W www.inkshed.co.uk

Jenny Rushton 175
Flat 9
12 Claremont Gardens
Surbiton, Surrey KT6 4TL
F 01483 283 007
M 07773 900 928
E jenny_rushton
@talk21.com
W www.contact-
me.net/JennyRushton

Brett Ryder 111
83b Paulet Road
Camberwell,
London SE5 9HW
T 020 7978 8131
F 020 7978 8131
E brettryder@
btconnect.com

Susan Scott 153,154
Flat 2/1
12 Yorkhill Street, Glasgow
Lanarkshire G3 8SB
T 0141 339 5170
F 0141 339 5170
M 07799 480 776
E susan.scott4
@btinternet.com
W www.scottish
illustrators.com
W www.photohall.com/
Susan_Scott/

Michael Sheehy 249
115 Crystal Palace Road
East Dulwich
London SE22 9ES
T 020 8693 4315
F 020 8693 4315
E michael.sheehy
@btinternet.com
A Central Illustration Agency
36 Wellington Street
London WC2E 7BD
T 020 7240 8925
E info@central
illustration.com
W www.central
illustration.com

Lorna Siviter 250
1 Nightingale Acre
Hatch Beauchamp
Taunton, Somerset TA3 6TF
T 01823 481 469
M 07789 812 333
E lornasiviter@mac.com
A Eastwing
98 Columbia Road
London E2 7QB
T 020 7613 5580
F 020 7613 2726
W www.eastwing.co.uk

Paul Slater 112
22 Partridge Close, Chesham
Buckinghamshire HP5 1LH
T 01494 786 780
F 01494 786 780
E paulslater@
btinternet.com
A Central Illustration Agency
36 Wellington Street
London WC2E 7BD
T 020 7240 8925
E info@central
illustration.com
W www.central
illustration.com

Andy Smith 21,22,23
A Private View Art Agency
T 01743 350 355
E create@pvuk.com
W www.pvuk.com

Philip Smith 176
Flat 4, Woodlands
263 Forest Road
Leytonstone
London E11 1LG
M 07790 282 030
E pgw.smith@
ukonline.co.uk

Nobby Sprouts 53
the dairy
5-7 Marischal Road
London SE13 5LE
T 020 8297 2212
F 020 8297 1680
M 07930 492 471
A the dairy studios
5-7 Marischal Road
London SE13 5LE
T 020 8297 2212
E thedairy@btclick.com
W www.thedairy
studios.co.uk

Julia Staite 177
27 Friars Walk, Southgate
London N14 5LR
M 07740 355 262
E jce_staite@hotmail.com

Jason Stavrou 113
Studio 357
Clerkenwell Workshops
27 Clerkenwell Close
London EC1 0AT
T 020 8470 0180
020 7251 5541
F 020 7251 5541
M 07989 364 648
E jason.stavrou
@virgin.net
W www.contact-
me.net/JasonStavrou
A Eye Candy Illustration
Agency, 15 Frobisher Court
Sydenham Rise
London SE23 3XH
T 020 8291 0729
T 01332 559 919
W www.eyecandy.co.uk

Anna Steinberg 251
6 Langler Road
London NW10 5TL
T 020 8964 1069
M 07890 882 252
E a.steinberg@
btopenworld.com

Deborah Stephens 252
7 George Court, Kings Place
Buckhurst Hill IG9 5HR
T 020 8504 6081
M 07798 828 123
E deborah@
dpsillustration.com
W www.dpsillustration.com

Helen Stephens 138
Flat 2, 295 King Street
London W6 9NH
T 020 8563 8919
F 020 8563 8919
E helen@stephens
pal.freeserve.co.uk

Andrew Steward 252
Flat 1, 15 Broadway Market
London E8 4PH
M 07775 838 133
E andy@interface-
newmedia.com
A The Organisation
Basement
69 Caledonian Road
London N1 9BT
T 020 7833 8268

Sharon Tancredi 178
8 Loraine Road
London N7 6EZ
T 020 7607 4340
M 07802 481 459
E s.tancredi@
btinternet.com

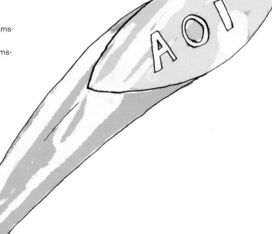